CHRISTIAN FOUNDATIONS
(REVISED)

CHRISTIAN FOUNDATIONS (REVISED)

An Introduction to Faith in Our Time

Kathleen Fischer
and
Thomas Hart

PAULIST PRESS
New York/Mahwah, N.J.

Acknowledgments

The Publisher gratefully acknowledges use of the following works:

"The Little Fish" and "The World of Religions" from the book SONG OF THE BIRD by Anthony de Mello, S.J., copyright © 1982 by Anthony de Mello, S.J. Reprinted by permission of Doubleday & Company, Inc.

"Who Am I?" from LETTERS AND PAPERS FROM PRISON by Dietrich Bonhoeffer, edited by Eberhard Bethge. Copyright © 1953, 1967, 1971 by SCM Press Ltd. Reprinted with permission of Macmillan Publishing Company.

Library of Congress Cataloging-in-Publication Data

Fischer, Kathleen R., 1940-
    Christian foundations : an introduction to faith in our time / by Kathleen Fischer and Thomas Hart.—Rev. ed.
        p.   cm.
    Includes bibliographical references and index.
    ISBN 0-8091-3595-7 (alk. paper)
    1. Theology. 2. Christian life—Catholic authors. I. Hart, Thomas N.
II. Title.
BT75.2.F564 1995   95-8989
230'.2—dc20   CIP

Published by Paulist Press
997 Macarthur Boulevard
Mahwah, New Jersey 07430

Printed and bound in the
United States of America

Contents

Introduction

One time on his way to the town of Gubbio, Francis of Assisi met a group of townspeople armed with clubs and sticks. "Where are you going?" he asked them.

"There is a fierce wolf which prowls around our town," they said. "He has attacked our animals and even our children. We are going to hunt him."

Francis went with the people. When they came upon the wolf, Francis said to them: "Let me talk to him." He walked up to the animal and extended his hand. The others drew back, certain that Francis was about to be devoured. But the wolf stood still and bowed his head. Francis patted him softly, saying:

"Come here, Brother Wolf. The people of the town have been telling me about you. You probably know that they fear and detest you. But I realize that you're hungry and that's what makes you do such terrible things. If you will agree to be peaceful, I promise that you will be fed for the rest of your days. Will you promise not to attack any more people or animals?"

To give his consent, the wolf placed his paw in Francis' hand. Francis then brought the animal to the city square and addressed the villagers: "Our brother wolf promises never to attack anything or anyone again, if you will just agree to feed him." The inhabitants of Gubbio, fascinated by what they had seen, promised to

1

do their part. From that time on, the wolf acted just like
a tame dog.

This story is in many ways a parable of our age. We live in
very challenging times. The problems of the modern world
seem overwhelming to many, and one of the most common
responses is violence against whatever the threat is perceived
to be. There once lived a man who responded to similar
challenges more in the manner of Francis of Assisi. The man
was in fact Francis' model and inspiration, Jesus of Nazareth.
His movement grew from the humblest beginnings. It is still
no overwhelming force in the world. Yet it may be the answer
to our problems. As British essayist G.K. Chesterton once
remarked: It is not that Christianity has been tried and found
wanting; rather, Christianity has been found difficult and
never been tried.

This book is written from a conviction regarding the
relevance of the Christian faith even as the wolf stands at the
door. In it we explore the foundations of Christian conviction and the way of life that flows from that conviction. We
hope to demonstrate the validity and usefulness of the
Christian proposal for our present situation. In developing
our themes, we have drawn on the most helpful insights of
many contemporary theologians, presenting their ideas
within our own synthesis. All of us together, drawing on the
riches of a 2000 year old tradition, try to relate the Christian
message to the conditions of modern life. We hope this
results in a theology at once solidly grounded and contemporary. It is also ecumenical, or addressed to Christians and
would-be Christians of every denomination, though our
Roman Catholic background will undoubtedly show in the
character of our presentation.

As an introduction, this book is an overview of the
major issues in the Christian life. It does not provide an in-
depth treatment of these topics, but it explains their basic

and most essential elements. We hope it will both deepen your understanding and whet your appetite for further exploration. It may also serve as an update for those instructed in the faith in decades past. We present our ideas in a format intended for study and discussion, with questions, exercises, and suggestions for further reading at the end of each chapter.

Our first chapter reflects on the deepest questions raised by human life, those experiences that constitute for us the riddle of existence. The remaining chapters show how Christian faith responds to various facets of this riddle. Chapters 2 and 3, on the existence of God and images of God, focus on core questions of faith, how we experience and describe the Transcendent. In Chapters 4 and 5 we move to the meaning of God's revelation in the bible and in the person of Jesus, who is the center of Christian life. Chapters 6 and 7 treat the meaning of the commitment of faith, as well as the challenge posed to faith by the mystery of suffering and evil. Chapters 8, 9, 10, and 11—on Christian existence, the church, spirituality, and care of the earth—describe the ways in which individuals and communities are called to live out the Christian message today. Chapter 12, on the end of the world, heaven, and hell, treats what Christians expect in the future. And since Christianity exists in a world of many different faith options, the final chapter assesses Christianity's place among the religions of the world.

CHAPTER 1

The Riddle of Existence

Americans live in the most prosperous country in the world. We enjoy an abundance of material goods and every modern convenience. Yet all is not well.

Many people are dependent on drugs of one kind or another. A large number of people are seeing therapists. Half our marriages end in divorce. Muggings and rapes make city streets unsafe, and our cars and homes are ransacked in our absence. Less visible but often more disturbing, verbal, physical, and sexual violence wreck the peace of family life. Our prisons are filled and overfilled. And in hospitals and nursing homes, many would like nothing so much as to die— yet they do not die.

THE RIDDLE OF THE EVIL

On a walk downtown any Sunday afternoon, you see many signs of the problems besetting human beings even in a prosperous culture. Solitary figures—older women, youths, alcoholics, older men—people the streets. Some seem mentally ill, others just lonely and forlorn. They ask you for spare change. They talk to themselves. Porno theaters, abandoned shops, and cheap hotels constitute their environment. Drug traffickers dot the scene if you know how to spot them. At the corners, smartly dressed young people of both sexes stand around looking for pickups. You will probably not walk here often. The scene is troubling.

You turn your steps to the college campus, a venue more beautiful where the movement of life is upward. There you find many people genuinely enjoying the challenges and rewards of academic pursuits and the social life of the university. Some have a strong sense of purpose, and clear plans for the future. Some are excited by the discovery of new friendships.

For others, though, things are not going that well. The social life of the campus does not seem to include them. They feel rejected and lonely. Others have found romance, but the relationships somehow generate more anguish than happiness. Some students are burdened with financial worries. Others are failing courses. Some are anxious about their chances in the job market, where the competition they have experienced in class just continues in another sphere.

This whole complex of problems beneath the surface produces a profound crisis of meaning for not a few who walk today's campus. Young and upwardly mobile though these students be, the pessimism of philosophers like Schopenhauer, Nietzsche, and Camus finds resonance in their own hearts. Alcohol and drugs are a significant part of college life, and though suicide is not commonplace, it is not unheard of either.

Your own life may be going better, or it may not. In either case, there are probably questions. Where am I going? What is life all about? Do I have any friends I can count on? If I died, would anybody really miss me? Can I change what I do not like in myself? Can I accept myself as I am? Is there any relief from the loneliness I feel? Shall I use drugs or alcohol, as so many do? What should I do with my sexuality? Is it possible to be happy? What do I want?

Human existence is indeed a riddle. As soon as you get beneath the surface of the world's functioning or of your own ordinary consciousness, you find a tangle of questions. To be a human person is to be a questioner, Karl Rahner, the eminent Roman Catholic theologian, reminds us. The deepest question of all is the question we are to ourselves. Our very life has a great big question mark right at the heart of it. To be human, Rahner says, is ever to be a seeker of answers and also to have discovered that no answer satisfies. Even the good answers just give rise to deeper questions.

THE RIDDLE OF THE GOOD

Life is by no means all bleak. We go hiking or camping amid mountains, lakes, and rivers, and are struck by the beauty of the world. Spring comes, the weather warms, and trees flower in pink and white. The birds are back, and squirrels scamper from tree to ground and back again in search of food. Television brings us within range of yet more gorgeous landscapes, and the marvelous creatures that inhabit them. It takes us also into the depths of the sea, where coral and fish of every description offer spectacular panoramas. What a beautiful world. And how beautiful the people who dwell there. They find one another in friendship, and give each other gifts. They fall in love, and their hearts flow with feeling. A baby is born, and everyone bends to look.

We go to a play, movie, or symphony, a ballet or an opera, and are stirred by these powerful expressions of the grandeur of the human. The movie *Fiddler on the Roof* depicts the solid goodness of the family and the enduring strength of love amidst all the challenges of life. Beethoven's great Choral Symphony expresses the agony and the ecstasy of human existence, the music's profound beauty making us marvel at the reaches of the human spirit. The plays of

Shakespeare, the poetry of Emily Dickinson, the paintings of Vincent Van Gogh, and the fiction of Toni Morrison touch the same depths and stir the same emotions. Where does all this beauty come from, this depth, this richness?

In the human community around us, we see persons of extraordinary heroism. The civil rights advocate, Martin Luther King, imbued with a vision for a renewed human society, marches courageously for justice, giving up his life in the long campaign. Mother Teresa of Calcutta moves quietly among the dying poor of India, ministering to their needs. Australian physician Helen Caldicott sets aside her medical practice and devotes all her energies to stopping the nuclear arms race before it is too late. Mohandas Gandhi fasts and tirelessly leads a nation in non-violent protest to throw off its oppression. He too sacrifices his life for the cause. Working on a smaller scale are many persons closer to home. Parents, grandparents, and other acquaintances show us quiet courage and dignity in the way they go about their tasks and deal with others. They are persons whom the years have made beautiful in their patience, wisdom, and love.

Where does all this goodness come from? Is it any less a wonder than the evil? Particularly when genuinely good and loving persons emerge from love-deprived and destructive backgrounds, is not the mystery of the goodness even more amazing than the evil?

THE RIDDLE OF THE CHALLENGES FACING US TODAY

Ours is the century of world consciousness. Communications make us aware of what is happening all around the globe. Many images impinge. Wars are in progress in several countries. Grinding poverty, with hunger, disease, and early death, is simply what life is for vast numbers of people.

Refugee camps are home to hundreds of thousands fleeing famine or war. Meanwhile other people have far more than they need, overconsume, and carelessly squander the earth's limited resources. Forests are razed, topsoil destroyed, waters polluted, the earth's very atmosphere slowly worn away. Nations continue to set aside vast public resources to build weapons of war. There are already more than enough on hand for the destruction of the whole world many times over, yet newer, deadlier ones are continuously devised.

A welter of new dilemmas face science and technology as they continue to develop at an astonishing pace. We can now discern the sex of a human fetus. We can say what diseases or handicaps it has. Parents are thus confronted with new and difficult choices. We can freeze sperm, ovum, or embryo, inseminate artificially, fertilize and perhaps even nurture new life outside the body. We are gaining genetic control over what sorts of human beings we might bring into the world. How do we decide? Is this even our business?

We can transplant organs, or supply for missing organs with sophisticated technology. Our life expectancy in the United States has doubled since the beginning of the twentieth century, and we can keep people alive almost indefinitely, conscious or unconscious, with artificial supports. Who is to decide when it is time to die, and on what basis? All kinds of mind-altering drugs are being produced for the relief of distress or for temporary euphoria. How are these to be used?

These developments reveal to us the dizzying heights and depths of our creative powers, and the staggering difficulty of our dilemmas. No generation of human beings has ever had so much power over its own destiny, or so much responsibility for the ongoing evolution of the world. How are we to use what we know and are learning, what we have made and will still create?

Blaise Pascal, French philosopher and scientist of the seventeenth century, was already musing on the contradictory dimensions of human existence when he characterized the human person as caught somewhere between grandeur and misery. We experience both, and puzzle over the source and significance of each of them. We are impressed at different times with the immense joy and the dreadful agony of living. We are forcibly struck by the surpassing value and yet also the apparent absurdity of life. The universe is a riddle, and we ourselves are the deepest puzzle of all.

In sum, is there any explanation for all the evil in the world, any help for coping with it, any power for overcoming or at least reducing it? Is there any explanation for all the goodness in the world, anyone to thank or worship for it, any reason to think it is the greater reality and meant to triumph? Is there any guidance available to us as we grapple with the dilemmas that face us at this moment in history, any values or norms that can help us with the decisions we have to make? Is there some truth that would ground an attitude of hope rather than despair as we look about ourselves?

The sorts of questions we have been asking constitute a sort of preamble to religion. They are the questions the great religions propose to address. Only if we have an appreciation for the questions can we appreciate or even be interested in the answers. That is why we have begun as we have. In this book we cannot cover all the answers offered by all the religions. We can cover only one, and that in an introductory way.

Our focus is on the basic answers to the riddle of existence offered by Christian faith.

SUMMARY

As we become aware of the world around us and of our own life within it, we are impressed with the riddle of it all. We find our minds filled with questions. Indeed, we ourselves are the deepest question of all.

There is the riddle of the evil, of all the suffering in the world and the struggle of life, of the widespread wrongdoing that darkens the face of the earth. Why is there so much evil?

There is the riddle of the good, of the great and glorious parts of life and the beauty of the world. The good is just as thought-provoking as the evil. Why is there so much goodness and beauty?

There is the riddle of the challenges facing us at this particular moment of history. These challenges cause many to despair. Are there grounds for hope? Are there values and norms that can guide us in the decisions we have to make? Is there any power greater than ourselves to which we can appeal for help?

We find ourselves mystified by both the grandeur and the misery of the human person. The riddle of existence is the preamble to religion. Embedded in it is the question of God.

Questions and Exercises

1. Name one way in which the riddle of existence has come home to you. How do you answer it?

2. Do you agree with the chapter's assertion that the riddle of the good is just as puzzling as the riddle of the evil? Explain your answer.

3. What questions of your own help you understand Rahner's claim that to be human is to be a question to oneself?

4. Why does a book on Christian foundations begin with a chapter on the riddle of existence?

5. Listen closely as other people talk, for evidence of Rahner's thesis that the human person is basically a questioner.

6. Interview two or three people to learn the various ways they cope with the riddle and challenge of existence.

CHAPTER 2

The Existence of God

The riddle of human existence raises the question of God, the most fundamental religious question. Is there a God?

Most people can recognize this question as their own, even if they might ask it in a different way. Is there some higher power, something that made the universe, something now in charge of this complex and confusing event we call the world? Is there someone who is interested in me and my life, someone who may be trying to get my attention, someone who might want my worship and obedience and possibly even my love? The question is momentous, since its answer has many ramifications for the way one lives. There are three possible answers to it: atheism, agnosticism, and theism (or belief in God). Let us examine each of these answers in turn, and see on what grounds each rests.

ATHEISM

Atheism holds there is no God. Atheists take this position for a variety of reasons. We will look briefly at the reasons given by four well-known modern thinkers.

1) Albert Camus

Probably the most common reason for atheism among people at large is the manifest fact of so much evil and suffering in the world. In the face of this misery and apparent chaos especially in the human world, the atheist cannot believe in the God of Christians, who is supposed to be both good and powerful. An eloquent twentieth century exponent of this position is Albert Camus, the French existentialist novelist, whose view of human existence is cogently expressed in the metaphoric titles of his works: *The Stranger, The Plague, The Rebel*. For Camus, everyone experiences existence as a stranger in the world, the whole of existence as a death-dealing plague, and the most appropriate response to the human condition as out-and-out rebellion. Camus shows empathy particularly for the suffering of children, which he simply cannot reconcile with the supposed reality of God.

2) Karl Marx

Another prominent exponent of atheism is the nineteenth century philosopher and economist Karl Marx, but his atheism rests on a different foundation. His reason for opposing the Christian religion of his culture was that he saw it as the principal obstacle to justice for all. Christianity, he said, has tended not only to accept the status quo, but even to offer divine justification for it. It has viewed riches as a sign of God's blessing, and counseled the poor to make the most of their sufferings while they waited for the reward that would be theirs in heaven. Christianity has not paid much attention to the conditions under which people live in this world, because it has seen the world as merely a stage on which people work out their eternal salvation. This is why Marx, who was so keenly aware of the sufferings of the laboring classes, hated the form of belief in God he knew, the Christianity of his culture. He called it "the opium of the people," because it lulled them into subservient acceptance. If society were to be restructured on a just basis, Marx believed, the Christian religion would have to be destroyed. Marx's brand of atheism is thus a militant antitheism.

3) Friedrich Nietzsche

Another militant antitheistic form of atheism is that of the nineteenth century German philosopher Friedrich Nietzsche. Nietzsche's principal reason for being atheistic was that he thought it was the only way human beings could be free. God is oppressive. Under God, human beings can only grovel, obey, and live in fear. If the human spirit is to expand so that people can express themselves in the ways they need and want to, the God hypothesis must be vigorously resisted. Nietzsche was particularly opposed to the Christian emphasis on humility and meekness as virtues. For him they were not virtues at all. He extolled human strength and assertiveness, and wanted to see a generation of what he called "superpersons," his vision of what could evolve if the God hypothesis were eliminated.

4) Sigmund Freud

The twentieth century founder of psychoanalysis, Sigmund Freud, articulated a psychological suspicion. He viewed "God" as a mere projection of human need. The world is a frightening place, and we feel weak and inadequate in face of it. Out of our psychic need, we project into the skies above a powerful father figure who will protect and care for us. We call him God. The God hypothesis has no other basis than this. A truly mature person, willing to face reality as it is, would set this illusion aside.

The four thinkers we have considered are important not

just for their direct influence on the God debate, but because they represent positions people of lesser renown often adopt out of their own reflections. Many people have wondered if God is not just a projection of their own psyche. Many people have felt stunned by their experience of evil and suffering in the world. Many people have questioned whether religion is friend or enemy of personal fulfillment and justice for all. So each of these positions has a certain reasonableness, and constitutes a challenge to faith.

Yet none of them disproves the existence of God. It is very difficult to disprove the existence of *anything*—cosmic rays, devils, or unidentified flying objects. It is especially difficult, probably impossible, to prove the nonexistence of so mysterious and elusive a reality as God. Arguments can call the supposed reality into doubt. But they cannot definitely rule it out.

AGNOSTICISM

This brings us to the second basic position on God, agnosticism. The root of the word is the Greek for "not knowing." An agnostic is a person whose answer to the God question is: "I simply don't know." He or she regards the evidence as too confusing, the testimonies too conflicting to allow a resolution. Possibly too, the whole question seems unimportant. Who cares whether there is a God or not? Life goes on pretty much the same either way. So the agnostic shelves the matter, at least for the time being.

Another common reason for agnosticism and even atheism is the sinfulness of the churches. People are repelled by the Christians they study or work with, by public figures who profess Christianity but betray its values, by the periodic revelation of serious scandals within the community of faith. The whole Christian movement seems at times hypocritical and self-serving. Thus, ironically, one of the great stumbling blocks to belief turns out to be believers.

Atheists and agnostics are sometimes portrayed as ignorant or evil people. The fact is, there have been and are many very intelligent and good atheists and agnostics. Sometimes they have been intelligent enough to reject or at least be dubious about the God who has been presented to them, which is not necessarily the true God. Many have also been courageous people. In times past, when nearly everyone was a Christian at least in name, it took great courage to profess one's atheism or agnosticism. Today when atheism and agnosticism are widespread and quite acceptable, it may take equal courage to profess one's belief in God.

Before we leave atheism and agnosticism, we might just note that not all human reluctance to believe in God stems from speculative considerations. Some of our resistance is practical. If I acknowledged the reality of God, I might have to change my life. And I may not want to. Blaise Pascal once put the matter succinctly to an agnostic friend: "You say that if you could believe in God, you would give up your pleasures. I rather think that if you were willing to give up your pleasures, you would believe in God."

But on what basis might a reflective person of the present century do so? To this we now turn our attention.

THE FOUNDATIONS OF THEISM, OR BELIEF IN GOD

Many people are as convinced of the reality of God as unbelievers are convinced of their positions. Trying to put the bases of theism into some kind of form will involve us in two steps: first, establishing a method or approach to the question, and then elaborating some of the actual reasons which persuade people God is real.

Two Principles Which Chart the Course

The nineteenth century philosopher and theologian, John Henry Newman, offers us a very useful framework within which to view all the arguments which can be advanced to support belief in God. Newman was familiar with the so-called proofs of the existence of God which philosophers before him had constructed. There was the proof from motion in the world, the proof from contingency, the proof from ascending orders of perfection, the proof from order in the world. There were other proofs too. We cannot elaborate them here, but Newman correctly noted that all of them were abstract and philosophical. As a pastor, Newman had used them in trying to convince those who came to him with doubts. He had used them to shore up his own faith, for, like most believers, he himself was subject to doubt. What disappointed him was that no matter how hard he worked to clarify and perfect these classical proofs, neither he nor those he talked with were convinced by the arguments. Not that they exactly found holes in them. It just seemed that you could think and think about them, and almost be convinced, and then suddenly be back again to wondering if the proof really proved. Newman said of the existence of God that it was the truth of which he was most deeply convinced, yet every time he tried to put his conviction in the form of a demonstration, the matter eluded him. Puzzled by the peculiar nature of the whole problem, Newman continued to seek a more adequate accounting for our belief in God. Finally he arrived at his theory of the convergence of probabilities.

He employed the analogy of a steel rod and a steel cable to illustrate the difference between coming at the problem of God with a proof and coming at it with a number of probable indicators. A proof was like a steel rod. A convergence of probabilities was more like a cable. A cable is composed of a number of strands, each weak in itself, which come together to constitute something as strong as a steel rod. As Newman saw it, we cannot get an unassailable proof for God's existence. We can only get probable indicators, or hints. But there are a great many of them, they show an amazing variety, and they all converge on the same conclusion. It is this convergence of diverse probabilities on the conclusion that God exists which constitutes for Newman the rational basis of our belief.

Another important contribution Newman makes to the discussion is to call attention to the peculiar kind of knowing involved here. He calls this way of knowing the "illative sense." The illative or inferential sense is our faculty of concrete, as opposed to abstract, reasoning. The classical proofs for the existence of God operate on the level of abstract reasoning, and can be put into ordered logical sequences called syllogisms. Newman accepts the validity of this kind of knowing and reasoning, but insists that there is another kind of knowing and reasoning that works in the concrete, reasoning from concrete particular to concrete particular, and forming conclusions it does not know exactly how it reached. By this illative sense, the gifted artist knows exactly where and with what pressure to apply brush or chisel, the gourmet cook knows how to blend ingredients, the defensive football player knows where the play is going before it gets there, and each of us knows in various life situations whom we can trust and whom we had better not. None of these bits of knowledge is a matter of logical reasoning. In each case, as a matter of fact, it is very hard to set forth how one knows what one knows.

There are strong affinities between what Newman calls the illative sense and what others have called intuition. Intuition can err, of course, but it can also be uncanny in its correctness, and by its aid we know crucial truths we cannot know in any other way. Newman's uncovering of this dimension of human knowing enabled him to explain how an unlettered person could hold an unshakable conviction of the reality of God, and could hold it on a rational basis, even if the person could not retrace the process by which he or she came to be so persuaded. This kind of knowledge is concrete and intuitive rather than abstract and speculative.

Experiences That Point to God

Having considered our method, let us look now at some of the evidences that lead us, whether by fully conscious or partly unconscious processes, to the belief that God exists. None of them constitutes a proof. Each is a hint, a pointer, a probable indicator. American sociologist of religion Peter Berger coins the phrase "signals of transcendence" to designate such evidences. The ones we will consider are cited by many different thinkers. After reviewing them, we will name some of today's leading theologians and the experiences each of them finds particularly persuasive.

1) This Massive Mystery of a World.

We get up in the morning and confront the massive fact of the world. It cries out for an explanation. How did all this come to be? Why does it exist? It does not matter whether one is wondering about the mere fact of the world, why there is something rather than nothing, or over its various intricate marvels, or over the deep conundrum of the daily life of humankind. Closest to home is the riddle of one's own life. None of it explains itself. Rather, it presents itself as a great mystery and cries out for an explanation.

2) The Experience of Beauty and Goodness.

We experience beauty and goodness, and joy in living. Not always, but often. It may come in the form of an ocean beach, a fire in winter's cold, a bed when we are exhausted, someone who welcomes us when we are forsaken. We may know the value of the good and beautiful things of life clearly only when we are told that we have six months to live, and find ourselves suddenly facing the prospect of losing it all. Granted the mystery of evil in the world, isn't the mystery of goodness equally baffling? Where do all the good and wonderful things come from? Who gives such marvelous gifts? G.K. Chesterton said he came to the faith principally because he was looking for someone to thank for the gift of life.

3) The Testimony of Conscience.

We feel ourselves bound by certain moral obligations. We feel peaceful and good when we obey them, troubled and guilty when we do not. Some of these obligations are a nuisance; they go contrary to immediate self-interest. Yet they exercise a claim on us which we cannot shake off. They seem to be a law imposed upon us by a power greater than ourselves.

Granted there are residues of our childhood conditioning which induce false guilt when we violate them. But even after we have peeled all these away (if we can) there remain some obligations which we know are not just a matter of childhood conditioning, which have an inexorable claim on us. We know, for example, that we must not steal or cheat. We know we must not kill. We know we must not take sexual advantage of another. Even if we can get away with such actions, we recognize them as wrong and know we are guilty. It is this experience which points to a greater power to which we are subject.

4) The Trustworthiness of Reality.

We find ourselves basically trusting reality, even though it is tricky and sometimes thwarts us. Science is based on this trust, and science works. Our projects and our ethical choices are based on this trust. For some reason we celebrate the new year, though we know not what it will bring. We celebrate each new birth, though life is filled with difficulties. We falter and doubt at times, but generally we throw ourselves into life as if there were meaning, purpose, and value in it all. Why? In our proverbs we attest that things will somehow work out, that tomorrow is another day. "Hope springs eternal in the human breast," the poet Alexander Pope proclaims. Why? In this hope there is an implicit act of trust in God. Only if God exists is there any basis for trust—any ground of meaning, value, or intelligibility, any goal. Trust in reality and religious faith are materially the same.

5) The Testimony of Time.

Belief in God has a lot of time on its side. The Hebrew scriptures record a period of almost 2000 years during which people believed in Yahweh, maker of the world and active presence in human events. The Christian epoch represents another 2000 years of belief in the God of the Jews, now known as the Father of Jesus the Christ. And this is just the biblical tradition. There are also the theistic religions of Africa, Asia, and America. We are looking at the experience of countless generations of human beings living in various circumstances. From the time of the Enlightenment in the eighteenth century, the demise of faith has been confidently predicted again and again as faith was judged to be incompatible with scientific sophistication. But faith has never died out. It wanes at times; but then it waxes again. Can something so universal and durable be based on unreality?

6) The Witness of Outstanding Human Beings.

It is not just a question of a long history. So many eminent individuals have believed. Great philosophers, learned historians, brilliant scientists have believed. Great artists have believed, and their religious experience has been the inspiration of their paintings, their music, their literature. People who have plumbed the depths of learning and experience far more deeply than we, have carried a deep conviction of the reality of the divine. Granted that other philosophers, historians, scientists, and artists have not believed. If religious faith had no real foundation, could any discerning individual believe? Could so many?

7) *The Spiritual Power of Faith-Filled Lives.*

We encounter persons who live out of a deep faith, and we are struck by the goodness and fruitfulness of their lives. They say it is their faith that makes them what they are. There are people, of course, whose professed faith does not make a recognizable difference, or whose religious convictions prompt them to positively destructive actions. But we are speaking of those persons we meet close up whose spiritual quality impresses itself forcibly upon us, whose lives seem to be genuinely transformed by something deep within manifested in the whole way they carry themselves. History adds even more striking examples—saints, whose heights of prayer and extraordinary self-giving pose a prodigious puzzle if there is no God. We would have to say they are deluded in what they are most convinced of, and leave their remarkable quality as human beings with the paltriest of explanations.

8) *Our Own Religious Experience.*

We come to our own experience. It may not have happened often, but perhaps we can recall certain occasions when we knew unmistakably that God was in us or near us or had just done something for us. A friend told us it happened to her as her first child was being born. Here was this tiny, perfectly formed living person emerging from her body, of her flesh yet not fashioned by her, presenting itself as an amazing, gratuitous gift. She remembered a profound sense of God—in the room, in her child, in herself.

Blaise Pascal recounts two strong religious experiences which produced his own conversion. The first occurred when a virulent illness threatened his life, the second when he slipped from the carriage in which he was riding and rolled right to the brink of a precipice. Both times he experienced his deliverance from death as miraculous, as an unaccountable embrace of love.

We once asked a young seminarian what had drawn him to his life choice. He told us he used to drive a big earthmover by day, and drink and engage in casual sex by night. That was his whole life, he said. One summer day just like any other summer day, as he was driving his earthmover under the hot sun, he suddenly felt God's love seize and hold him. It lasted several minutes, and he felt its powerful sway the rest of the day. The experience was a total surprise, the last thing he expected ever to happen to him. He was so deeply moved and so changed that he felt he had to respond to it with his whole life.

Each person's religious experiences are different. They do not constitute a proof for anyone else. But to the person experiencing them, they carry strong internal conviction, often potent enough to change a whole life direction.

Some Prominent Contemporary Theologians

In arguing for the reality of God, many theologians rely principally on certain human experiences which they regard as universal. We close out our consideration by looking at three of these.

1) Karl Rahner: God at the Edges of Consciousness.
Karl Rahner holds that the existence of God is in a way quite evident, because there is always a peripheral experience

of God included in the experience of anything else. Rahner invokes the metaphor of the horizon to describe this constant unobtrusive experience of God. We do not directly see the horizon, and we rarely advert to it. But it is the backdrop against which we see everything else. Similarly, we do not see God, and may rarely advert to God. But God is the horizon against which we see everything else, and thus God is always at the fringes of our awareness.

Rahner suggests that we can recognize this experience if we substitute the term "mystery" for the term "God," for ultimately that is what God is. Whatever it is that holds our attention at any given moment, we are at least dimly aware of the mystery that surrounds it. We wonder about it. If it is good, we are attracted to it yet also aware that it does not satisfy us. We look beyond it. Whatever answers we find to our questions, we are aware of their limitations, and yearn for more adequate answers. Everything is a puzzlement, something of a disappointment, a hint, a lure. That *beyond* into which we look with both curiosity and longing, that backdrop or horizon against which the limitations of everything in this world are exposed, is the mystery we call God.

2) Rosemary Radford Ruether: God the Empowering Matrix.
American Roman Catholic theologian Rosemary Radford Ruether uses a different metaphor to heighten our God-awareness. A feminist theologian mindful of the destructiveness of the arbitrary masculinizing of God, Ruether wants to change what she sees to be the prevalent God-image, "God the paternal superego," to "God the empowering matrix." We are all familiar with God as father, and only slightly less familiar with God as judge (superego), both masculine images. Ruether's most basic experience of God is a different one. She is most struck by the deep-down goodness of reality and the fecundity of nature. For her, God is the one who liberally brings forth, supports, and empow-

ers. A matrix, derived from the Latin word for mother, is the ground in which things are embedded or within which they are contained. In this maternal metaphor, Ruether envisions God as the fertile seedbed in which we and all other things are rooted.

3) Paul Tillich: God in the Depth of Things.

Protestant theologian Paul Tillich takes yet another approach to God. He finds God in the depth of all reality. God is the ground of being, he often says, or God is the depth in things. If you do not think you have any experience of God, Tillich suggests, forget the word "God" and ask yourself where you experience depth. That is where you contact the mystery of God. Is it in a love relationship with someone? Is it in profound loneliness? Is it in the awesome beauty of a rose, a child, a piece of art? Is it in the mystery of sexuality? Is it in the radical contingency of your life? Where you experience depth, there you touch God, for God is the depth in things. Things go downward into God the more we get below their surfaces and uncover layer by layer their depths. God is the profound mystery at the bottom of them, partly revealed through them.

CONCLUDING OBSERVATIONS

There are many more theologians and more evidences and arguments put forward by various thinkers for the existence of God. We have not reviewed them all, but we have studied a sufficient sample, it is hoped, to show that belief in God does have grounds in experience and reflection.

Methodologically, we took our cue from Newman. Rather than try to take some single line of evidence and develop it into an unassailable proof, we acknowledged the merely probable character of the evidence but noted its impressive abundance and variety. Many diverse probable indicators converge on the same conclusion, like countless small strands of steel forming a cable.

It may seem a shame that in a matter of such moment we have to rely on mere probability. Newman reminds us that in most, if not all, the important matters of life we have to rely on probability because that is all we can get. We do it every time we make a purchase, even as major a purchase as a car or home. We do it when we choose a school, a course, a job. We do it when we enter a relationship, even so consequential a relationship as marriage. Always we are risking, taking as informed and reflective a chance as possible, but taking a chance nevertheless. We can refuse to play the game, but that too is a gamble.

There is an important characteristic about the sorts of evidences and experiences we have examined. In most of them, God is given in the experience itself, and we are already relating to God in the experience. We do not begin with something in experience, make a logical deduction to something outside it, and then try to establish a relationship with that. The experience is more like that recounted in a little story from the Orient.

> "Excuse me," said one ocean fish to another. "You are older and more experienced than I. Tell me, where can I find this thing they call the Ocean? I've been searching everywhere."
>
> "The Ocean," said the older fish, "is what you are swimming in now. This is it!"
>
> "This? But this is only water. I'm searching for the Ocean." And the young fish swam away to continue the search.

When we experience the promptings of conscience, we are already relating to God. When we are conscious of the depth in things, we are already in the presence of God. When we feel ourselves beckoned by reality to give ourselves in trust and invest in it, we are experiencing the beckoning of God. When we know the insufficiency of everything and restlessly long for something more, our spirits are already groping into the mystery of God. When we encounter a genuinely spiritual person, it is God we encounter in that person. When in a special moment we are unexpectedly loved or forgiven or rescued, it is at bottom God who embraces us. This means that the grounds on which we come to believe are the same grounds on which we live the relationship with God. We do not come to faith once and for all, and then dispense with the experiences that brought us there. Our faith is again assailed by doubt, and again the experiences buttress and nourish it. Faith is an ongoing commitment in trust, obedience, and gratitude to the God who relates to us in our daily experience.

SUMMARY

In this chapter we have raised the question of the existence of God, a question that arises in our minds as we contemplate the riddle of life. People give the question one of three answers: atheism, agnosticism, or theism. Camus, Marx, Nietzsche, and Freud are modern exponents of atheism, each with his own reason, reasons with which many can identify. Agnosticism is content to leave the question unanswered, because it is judged difficult, irrelevant, or threatening. Both atheism and agnosticism find grounds for disbelief in the lives of believers.

Theism is able to adduce many evidences and experiences in support of its belief that God exists, several of them briefly sketched here. Newman counsels us to trust our informal, intuitive reasoning rather than try to build some logical proof, and to notice the rich variety of probable indicators that point to the reality of God. We noted that God is given in the experiences themselves, so that the bases of our faith are also the grounds of the lived relationship.

Questions and Exercises

1. What is atheism? Name some of its leading exponents and summarize the arguments they offer.
2. What is agnosticism, and what is its rationale?
3. Explain the contributions John Henry Newman has made to our understanding of the rational bases of our belief in God's existence.
4. What are some of the evidences and experiences which ground theism's affirmation of the existence of God?
5. Name the chief evidences and experiences which support your own belief in God, or the evidences and experiences that persuade you there is no God.
6. In a dialogue with an atheist, agnostic, or theist of your acquaintance, try to discover why they hold what they do and how it influences their lives.
7. See if you can find instances of Newman's illative sense, or informal concrete reasoning, at work in some areas of your life other than the religious.

Suggestions for Further Reading

Karen Armstrong, *A History of God: The 4000 Year Quest of Judaism, Christianity, and Islam* (Ballantine, 1993). A British scholar's tracing of the history of how men and women have perceived and experienced God from Abraham to the present.

Peter Berger, *A Rumor of Angels* (Doubleday, 1990). A brief but provocative exploration of "signals of transcendence" in ordinary experience.

G.K. Chesterton, *Orthodoxy* (Doubleday, 1959). A convert and gifted writer's concrete and personal argument for the existence of God and the truth of Christianity.

Paul Davies, *The Mind of God: The Scientific Basis for a Rational World* (Simon and Schuster, 1992). A contemporary scientist argues from intricate patterns in the universe to the mind of God.

Hans Küng, *Does God Exist?* (Crossroad, 1994). A comprehensive review of atheism's main exponents and their arguments, along with the counter-case for God.

John Henry Newman, *A Grammar of Assent* (Doubleday, 1955). A philosophical essay on modes of human knowing, which contains many of Newman's key ideas on the God question.

Blaise Pascal, *Pascal's Pensees* (Penguin, 1966). A famous philosopher's musings on the theistic implications of ordinary experience.

CHAPTER 3

Images of God

What is your image of God? How does it compare with some of the popular images? There is the judge in the sky, who sees all evildoing and keeps a record of it for judgment day. There is the great watchmaker, who set the universe in motion and keeps it running. There is the distant blissful one, dwelling in a cloud of light, untouched by the pain and conflict of the world. There is the benign bearded old man who makes the laws and takes care of everyone. There is Jesus, the human face of God.

Where do these images come from? Why do we have images at all? They originate from the fact that no one has ever seen God. Many people say they have *experienced* God. We ourselves may have felt the presence of God or discerned something of the activity of God in the world. But God remains a mystery, beyond the reach of our eyes and the comprehension of our minds. So when it comes to God, we have to use our imaginations. On the basis of our religious experience, we form images of God and tell stories of God's activities, images and stories more or less adequate to the mystery they attempt to describe.

The bible began this activity long ago. On the basis of their experience of God, the Hebrews formed images of God and told stories describing God's action in the world. On the basis of his experience, Jesus shared images of God with his contemporaries and told stories of God. It is interesting that the bible never gives a definition or any philosophical description of God. It speaks to us rather in the language of the imagination—images, metaphors, and stories.

However inadequate they may be because of the surpassing mystery of God's being, our images of God are extremely important in our lives, for it is through them that we relate to God. It is partly because of our images of God that we feel good about ourselves or bad, secure or fearful, close to God or distant, intolerant of others or accepting. So it is a matter of the highest practical importance that our images of God be as adequate as they can be.

It is the bible that serves Jews and Christians as the norm for the adequacy of their God-images. We form our images of God in a kind of movement back and forth between the experiences of God reported in the bible and our own contemporary experiences. In this chapter we will explore the different ways the bible images God. Then we will reflect on the implications of this varied imagery. Finally, we will try to probe the meaning of the Christian doctrine of the Trinity.

BIBLICAL IMAGES OF GOD

In its presentation of the mystery of God, the bible uses both personal and impersonal images, and the personal ones are sometimes masculine and sometimes feminine. We will look first at the masculine, then the feminine, then the impersonal images.

Male Images

The biblical images most familiar to us are male. The bible calls God King, Lord, Master, Warrior, Husband, and Judge; and Jesus' favorite name for God is Father.

These ways of imaging God arose from the Hebrew life experience. They knew God as King of the universe and Lord of history, something like, though much greater than, their own kings or the kings of other nations. They imagined God as a great Warrior, because they had to fight many battles to win their place in the promised land, and they saw God as leading them to victory. They called God "Lord of Hosts," meaning General of armies. They also knew God as Lawgiver, because they saw their law as the expression of God's will for their lives. Through their experience of God's protection of them as a people, they came to view God as a kind of great Shepherd, after the analogy of their own shepherds.

The prophet Hosea introduced another image of God, and it became prominent in Hebrew consciousness ever after that. It was the image of God as Lover or Husband. God was seen as having entered into a sort of marital covenant with his people when he gave them the law. He pledged his fidelity to them, and demanded their fidelity in return. God is pictured as wooing his people as a man woos a woman, and being grieved by their subsequent sinfulness as a husband would be grieved by his wife's infidelity or rejection. This is an image of tender, intimate loving, and of a deep personal investment in human beings on God's part.

Jesus uses many of these, his people's, images for God, but the image he employs most is one that was not very common in Hebrew usage: Father. Jesus refines even this portrayal, making it more intimate: He calls God "Abba." This is what Hebrew children called their fathers, its closest English equivalent being "Daddy" or "Papa." The term expresses the extraordinary closeness Jesus felt with God. Dutch Roman Catholic theologian Edward Schillebeeckx sees this image as expressing the very heart of Jesus' religious experience, and the ultimate source of the way Jesus preached and embodied God's attitude to human beings.

Jesus invites his followers into this same sort of intimate relationship with God.

These are some of the male images the bible employs to describe the Mystery. It is not surprising that male images predominate in the bible, because Hebrew culture was patriarchal and the biblical writers were mostly if not all men. These images have so dominated popular consciousness that most people think of God as in some sense really male. When God is spoken of with pronouns, "he" and "him" are the ones usually used. The reactions one gets when using a female or impersonal pronoun show how deeply entrenched and identified with supposedly objective truth these male imaginings are.

Female Images

What is often overlooked is that the bible also uses female images for God. We owe a debt of gratitude to the women's movement for bringing this back to our awareness.

God the creator is sometimes depicted as a woman giving birth, and Christ and the Holy Spirit are sometimes depicted in female images as well. Deuteronomy 32:18 uses a reproductive image of God as both male and female, saying to the people: "You forgot the Rock who begot you, unmindful now of the God who gave you birth." Job 38:28-29 uses the same sort of dual imagery, speaking of God's fathering of the rain and birthing of the ice from her womb. The same chapter speaks of the sea "leaping tumultuous from the womb." The prophet Isaiah depicts God suffering labor pains trying to bring forth a people who live justly:

> From the beginning I have been silent,
> I have kept quiet, held myself in check.
> I groan like a woman in labor,
> I suffocate, I stifle (Is 42:14).

Paul, in his speech to the Greeks in the Areopagus, says that God is not far from any of us, for "in God we live and move and have our being" (Acts 17). Though Paul does not explicitly name the womb here, at no other time in human experience except during gestation do we exist within another person. Jesus at the last supper implies that his suffering to bring forth the new humanity could be compared to the pangs of a woman in labor, in sorrow because "her hour has come" (Jn 16:21), as had his own. Paul uses similar imagery of his own ministry: "I must go through the pain of giving birth to you all over again, until Christ is formed in you" (Gal 4:19). He employs the same metaphor when he speaks of God's salvation as a birthing process which occurs within the individual as well as in creation at large:

> From the beginning till now the entire creation, as we know, has been groaning in one great act of giving birth; and not only creation, but all of us who possess the first fruits of the Spirit, we too groan inwardly as we wait for our bodies to be set free (Rom 8:22).

John's gospel speaks of our being "born of God" (Jn 1:12), and his first letter reaffirms that everyone who loves is "born of God" (4:7), a usage echoing Jesus' own insistence that a person must be born again to enter the kingdom of God (Jn 3:3). Since it is not common to speak of anyone being born of a man, it does not seem unreasonable to view all "new birth" or "born again" images in scripture as a female imaging of God.

Feminine images abound also in the bible's description of God's ongoing nurturance of us. Hosea depicts God as a loving parent teaching a child to walk, and stooping down to give a child food, offices that would have been performed by the mother in Hebrew culture (Hos 11:1-4). Second Isaiah adds a nursing image:

> Does a woman forget the baby at her breast,
> or fail to cherish the child of her womb?
> Yet even if she forget,
> I will never forget you (Is 49:15).

The psalmist gives us an image of repose:

> I am not concerned with great affairs,
> or marvels beyond my scope.
> Enough for me to keep my soul tranquil and quiet,
> like a child in its mother's arms,
> as content as a child that has been weaned (Ps 131).

Jesus continues this female portrayal as he tries to describe God's concern for the sinner. His image is that of a woman tirelessly sweeping for her lost coin, for money that is terribly important to her (Lk 15). In the same vein, he depicts himself as a hen trying to gather her chicks under her wings and being refused (Lk 13).

A much used and very significant image for God in the Hebrew scriptures is that of Sophia or Lady Wisdom. "Wisdom" is a feminine noun both in Hebrew and in Greek, and in the bible is often *personified* as a woman to express how God is graciously present and salvifically active in the world on behalf of human beings. Lady Sophia seeks people out, finds them on the road, invites them to dinner. Called sister, mother, wife, she offers life, rest, knowledge, and salvation to those who accept her. She is described as intelligent and all-powerful (Wis 7:22), a people-loving spirit (Prov 8:3; Wis 1:6) who shares the throne of God (Wis 9:10). She is an initiate of God's knowledge, an associate in God's works (Prov 8:30), an emanation of the God of light, an image of God's goodness (Wis 7:26). In the Christian scriptures, when Jesus' contemporaries notice how compellingly he fulfills this portrait in his own person and work, they identify him with this personified wisdom tradition (e.g., Lk 7:35; 1 Cor 1:24).

For many theologians and saints in subsequent Christian history, female images for God and even Christ have played an important role. Some of the men in whose writings these images appear are Clement of Alexandria, St. John Chrysostom, St. Ambrose, St. Gregory of Nyssa, St. Augustine, the Venerable Bede, St. Anselm, St. Thomas Aquinas, and St. Bonaventure. Among women who write in this vein are St. Catherine of Siena, St. Bridget of Sweden, Julian of Norwich, and St. Teresa of Avila.

Impersonal Images

The other dimension of the biblical imaging of God which is often overlooked is the bible's use of impersonal images for God. These abound in the psalms, where God is described as Rock, Shield, Fortress (Ps 18, 62), Water (Ps 42, 63), Mountain (Ps 121), Light (Ps 27), and where the psalmist speaks of "taking shelter in the shadow of God's wings" (Ps 36), as if God were a great protecting bird. In other places in the bible, God is depicted as thunder (Ex 19), a gentle breeze (1 Kgs 19), fire (Heb 12), bread (Jn 6).

The mere making of such a list does not begin to bring out the power of these impersonal images for God. One must take these metaphors one by one and let them work on the imagination. Then we can see how some dimensions of God's reality and relationship to us are better expressed in impersonal than in personal images. This gives us a better feel for those religions which have preferred to speak of the ultimate mystery predominantly in impersonal imagery. They are not as far from the biblical tradition as might at first appear.

As with the feminine, the impersonal images too are carried on in Christian tradition. St. Catherine of Siena describes God as a ray of love, a ray of darkness, a calm sea. Other mystics see God as a flame or river of fire which fills the universe. The well-known scientist, theologian, and mystic of the twentieth century, Pierre Teilhard de Chardin, sees the presence of God in the world as rays of light suffusing all matter. St. John of the Cross, continually purified through his long experience with God, ends by rejecting all the usual images and preferring to call God *nada*, Spanish for "nothing." The presence of God was for him a kind of absence.

In retreats and workshops, we have often invited people to do an exercise involving images of God. Without any of the foregoing preparation, we ask them to relax, close their eyes, and just let their imaginations offer to awareness some symbol for God. Then we have them spend some time interacting with that symbol. It is amazing the variety of images which spontaneously arise. Some see the face of a child, some the face of a suffering poor woman, some a serene lake. Some see Jesus, some the face of their wife, husband, or best friend. Some visualize a mountain, a circle of light, or a fish. People often express surprise that it is not a "religious" image such as Father, or Jesus, or a cross that came to their minds, but rather something quite "secular." The exercise brings out the point that God is revealed in many places in ordinary experience, that anything might symbolize God because everything does, and that most individuals have certain favorite images.

It should not be surprising that in such an exercise the faces of parents, spouses, or best friends come to mind. For in the book of Genesis, God says: "Let us make humankind in our image, after our likeness" (Gen 1:26). It would seem, then, that among all created things, human beings are the best symbols of God, and therefore also important avenues of our religious experience. This is the deeper grounding of the experience which Jesus' disciples had in their acquaintance with this particular man from Nazareth: In his universal love and his desire to help, he seemed to them to express what God is.

And so the letter to the Colossians calls him "the image of the invisible God" (1:15), and Hebrews "the exact representation of the Father's being" (1:3).

Before leaving this exploration of biblical images of God, we should note that the bible often describes God by telling stories of God. The stories exhibit the same sort of variety as the images do. There is the story of God calling Abraham and Sarah and leading them to the land of promise. There is the story of God bringing the Hebrews out of Egypt, and delivering them from their pursuing slaveowners in the encounter at the sea. There are the stories of God protecting and feeding the people in the desert. Without trying to delineate the nature of God, the bible stories capture the fundamental Hebrew experience of God: God is the one who cares and saves.

Jesus continues the story-telling tradition. His parables present images of God in action. God is the sower who sows good seed (Mt 13). God is the gracious host who invites everyone to a banquet (Lk 14). God is the vineyard owner who pays his workers very generously (Mt 20). God is the compassionate father who welcomes back his wayward son (Lk 15). God is the vinedresser, carefully pruning vines so that they will bear more fruit (Jn 15). Jesus does not define God either. He just paints pictures.

IMPLICATIONS OF THE BIBLICAL IMAGING OF GOD

What emerges clearly from a study of the bible's imaging of God is that there is obviously no one image which says it all. The biblical authors evidently feel a need to employ a great many images of different sorts, to express various facets of a mystery that transcends all imaging. Each image embodies a partial insight. Even if we put them all together, we still have not comprehended the mystery.

When we lose sight of this fact and confuse the image with the reality, we fall into idolatry, for we have taken something less than God for God. The bible is emphatic on this point. Among the commandments God gives, one is that the people should make no graven image of their God as the other nations do. Why? Because it is so easy to forget that an image is just an image, and to begin to confuse it with the reality itself. In an earlier encounter with God, when Moses asks the divine name so that he can give the people a better idea who it is they are dealing with, God answers in these terms: "Tell the people 'I am' sent you" (Ex 3:14). This statement eloquently protects the divine mystery.

One of the ways an individual or a culture can lapse into idolatry without realizing it is to use exclusively male metaphors for God, and speak of God always as "he" or "him." When the same image is presented over and over, it is much easier to confuse it with the reality. One of the deleterious effects of male imaging only is a subtle reinforcement of sexism, for if God is male, perhaps it is appropriate that there be male dominance in human society as well.

There is a further difficulty. An exclusively masculine presentation of God limits the ways we can relate to God. Some persons find King, Lord, and Judge uninteresting and uninspiring images, perhaps even repugnant. Such images do not correspond with their experience of God, and so do not illumine or nourish their faith lives. Other persons' experience of father in human terms has been almost entirely painful. It is very hard for them to relate with any confidence or warmth to a God portrayed in exclusively fatherly terms. When they are reminded that the bible uses female and impersonal images for God as well, they feel liberated, their capacities for relating to God immensely expanded.

GOD AS TRINITY

One of the dogmas or doctrines (both terms mean "teaching") of Christianity is that God is trinitarian or triune, i.e., that there is some kind of "threeness" in the one God. This doctrine of "three persons in one God," Father, Son, and Holy Spirit, strongly influences how Christians think about God.

Karl Rahner makes two intriguing observations about most Christians vis-à-vis the Trinity. The first is that although most Christians believe the doctrine because it has been taught them, it makes no real difference to their life of faith. They think of God and pray to God as one. What they imagine as they do so is either God as Father or else God as Jesus. Rahner's aim is to resuscitate the relevance of the Trinity for the Christian life. Another preliminary observation he makes is that most Christians, when asked to say what the doctrine means, show themselves to be what he calls "tritheists," i.e., believers in three Gods. This is natural enough, he says, as this is what happens when the imagination processes the doctrine as usually verbalized, "three persons in one God." Yet tritheism is far from what the doctrine intends. Rahner seeks to recover the original meaning of the doctrine so that it is not an unnecessary stumbling block to faith.

The confusion, he explains, turns on the word "person." The doctrine of the Trinity was originally formulated in Greek in the early Christian centuries. The English word "person" as we use it today means an independent center of consciousness and freedom. That is not the meaning of the original Greek terms *hypostasis* and *prosopon*. The meaning of these technical terms in Greek philosophy is difficult to render in English today. "Subsistence" comes close, but because subsistence is not a common term it does not convey much meaning to us. Rahner suggests "way of being" as a better translation. Thus the doctrine of the Trinity in meaningful English might be put this way: The one God has three ways of being. It was never the intent of the doctrine to say that God has three centers of consciousness and freedom, three "personalities."

It is very important to remember, Rahner says, that trinitarian thinking began not as a piece of speculation about God, but as the expression of the *religious experience* of the followers of Jesus. They experienced God in an incarnate or historically concrete way in Jesus, and they experienced God in a spiritual way in the depth of their own spirit. They called the first experience the "Son" and the other the "Holy Spirit." The mystery that remains ever in the background, the mystery to which Son and Spirit pointed, they called the "Father," as Jesus did. It is of the Father that John's gospel says: "No one has ever seen God. The only-begotten Son, who is in the bosom of the Father, has made God known" (Jn 1:18).

Thus, there is only one God, and this God remains always mystery to us, even in revelatory experience. Yet God cares for us, and so we call God "Father" (loving parent). How do we know God's care? Because of God's gracious out-reach to us in Son and Spirit. The encounter with God incarnate in Jesus corresponds to our bodiliness: We can see, touch, and hear God incarnate. The encounter with God as Spirit corresponds to the spiritual dimension of our being: we experience God as Spirit in the depths of our own spirit, present to us, grounding our faith, hope, and love, endowing us with spiritual gifts for the help of others (1 Cor 12 and 13), making Father and Son present (Jn 15:23), praying in us with unspeakable groanings (Rom 8:26-27), reminding us of the things Jesus said and teaching us their meaning (Jn 16:12-14), uniting us with other believers in the social body called church (1 Cor 12:12-13). In sum, we experience God as one, yet as having three distinguishable ways of being. This is the basis of Christianity's trinitarian presentation of God.

American theologian Catherine Mowry LaCugna, who does an exhaustive study of the history of trinitarian theology, is at one with Rahner in emphasizing that the doctrine of the Trinity has important implications for our relationship with God. It expresses how a God of gracious love takes the initiative in inviting us into communion with self through Christ in the Holy Spirit. The Trinity is thus the central symbol of God's love for us. In addition, it has ramifications for the way we structure human society. LaCugna stresses the intrinsic meaning of person as a relational way of being. The doctrine of the trinitarian persons tells us that God's being is by nature relational. Trinitarian communion is not something that is added on after the one God is described; God is relational through and through, so that at the very heart of divine mystery is community. For LaCugna, the image of God in humanity is therefore found not in the solitary self, but in persons who are in authentic communion with others. The Trinity serves as a model for human relationships, inasmuch as it shows us a community of persons bound together in relationships of mutuality and equality. LaCugna and other feminist theologians stress that relationships of mutuality and equality in diversity are precisely what our societies and the earth need, and what God calls us to in Christ.

Anglican theologian D.M. Baillie draws out the significance of Trinity by joining two ideas in a fresh way. What is distinctive, he asks, about the Christian God as opposed to the God of other religions? He says one of two answers is usually given: The Christian God is trinitarian, or the Christian God is love. Baillie credits both answers, then points out that they amount to the same thing. The doctrine of the Trinity *means* that God is love, i.e., that God chooses not to remain self-enclosed, but to reach out graciously to humankind in Son and Spirit.

On this understanding the doctrine of the Trinity ceases to be abstract, philosophical speculation about something which has little to do with us except as a dogma to be learned and believed. Now we understand it as an articulation of the way we actually experience the graciousness of the mystery we call God. It serves as the basis of our own graciousness in relationship.

But there remains a problem of language. Our chief daily contact with the trinitarian image of God is the sign of the cross. In the sign of the cross as usually articulated, we have an all-male God: Father, Son, and (relatively non-descript) Holy Spirit, which reinforces sexism. Feminists offer us liberating alternatives such as: In the name of the Creator, and of the Liberator, and of the empowering Spirit. Amen.

SUMMARY

How shall we describe the God we have experienced but not seen? The transcendent mystery of God, always beyond our grasp, can only be presented in images which fall short of the reality they try to express.

Images and stories are the language of the bible itself, which addresses itself more to our imaginations than to our conceptual intellects. The bible uses impersonal as well as personal images, female as well as male. Christian mystics and theologians have generally kept this richness of imagery alive through the ages, in their personal prayer lives and in their teaching. Dogmatic theology and popular catechesis have done less well.

The best safeguard against absolutizing and hence idol-izing any particular image of God is to follow the biblical example of using a rich variety of images. The benefits are considerable both for the individual and for the culture at large.

The Christian doctrine of the Trinity, or some sort of threeness in God, has certainly influenced the way Christians imagine God. LaCugna draws out the implications in terms both of God's love for us and of our relationships with one another. Rahner suggests speaking of God's three "ways of being" rather than of three "persons" in God, to avoid imaginative distortions of the original idea. Baillie shows how God as trinitarian and God as love are different expressions of the same idea.

Questions and Exercises

1. What role do images of God play in the biblical presentation of God? What sorts of images are offered?

2. Are Christians bound to think of God as Father? Is Father the most adequate image for God?

3. What is the meaning of the Christian doctrine of the Trinity?

4. Why are there so many images of God? What are some of the harmful effects of relying on just one or two images?

5. Try the exercise described in the chapter: Relax, close your eyes, and let your imagination present you with a symbol for God. Interact with that symbol as you feel moved to, e.g., speak to it or let it speak to you. When you have finished the exercise, reflect on the experience.

6. Try using feminine images of God in your prayer and in your talk about God, and notice what effect it has. Try the same thing with impersonal images.

7. After some brief explanation, try speaking of God in feminine or impersonal terms in group prayer or theological discussion, and then ask participants to share their reactions.

Suggestions for Further Reading

Avery Dulles, *Models of Revelation* (Orbis, 1992). A survey and critique of the chief models employed for understanding the experience of divine revelation.

Virginia Fabella and Mercy Amba Oduyoye, eds., *With Passion and Compassion: Third World Women Doing Theology* (Orbis, 1988). Explores questions of religious language within a global context.

Robert Hood, *Must God Remain Greek?* (Fortress, 1990). A theology professor frees God from Graeco-Roman roots and pleads for a transcultural theology penetrated by the spirituality of Africa and the Caribbean.

Elizabeth Johnson, *She Who Is: The Mystery of God in Feminist Theological Discourse* (Crossroad, 1992). Presents arguments from the bible and tradition for the need and legitimacy of presenting God in female images.

Catherine Mowry LaCugna, *God for Us: The Trinity and Christian Life* (HarperSanFrancisco, 1991). A comprehensive historical and theoretical analysis restoring the doctrine of the Trinity to the heart of Christian life.

Sallie McFague, *Models of God: Theology for an Ecological, Nuclear Age* (Fortress, 1987). Explores the biblical tradition of imaging God, and argues for models which reflect both ecological sensitivity and concern for justice.

Sandra Schneiders, *Women and the Word* (Paulist, 1986). Suggests some ways of resolving the traditional ascription of masculinity to God, both faithful to tradition and liberating.

Brian Wren, *What Language Shall I Borrow? God-Talk in Worship* (Crossroad, 1989). A poet and hymn-maker reflects on the importance of God images, and provides a variety of fresh images for use in worship.

CHAPTER 4

The Bible

The bible remains, year after year, the best selling book in the world. It has been translated from the original languages of its composition—Hebrew, Aramaic, and Greek—into practically every language known to humanity. It has spawned whole libraries of commentary, libraries which continue to grow at an astonishing rate. In fact, the bible has probably never enjoyed such intense study as it does in our own day, both by scholars and by believers at large.

Why is this book so important? For several reasons. It serves as the foundation of two of the world's major religions, Judaism and Christianity. It is reverenced by Islam as the historical and prophetic background for God's definitive prophecy in Muhammed. Jews believe their scriptures to be God's revelation to them, and through them to all humankind. Christians believe both the Jewish scriptures and especially their own New Testament to be God's revelation to them, and through them to all humankind. This exalted status of revelation, or inspired word of God, accords the bible a place of unique eminence for those who believe. They turn to it again and again for inspiration, for the values and purposes that govern their lives, for religious instruction and exhortation, for personal meditation and liturgical celebration. The bible is also the principal source for theology.

The word "bible" derives from the Greek word *biblia*, which means "books." The term is apt because the bible is not a single book but a collection of books written by many different authors over time. It contains a considerable variety of theological viewpoints. This is why it is simplistic to ask, "What does the bible say about such and such?" A better question would be, "What do the books say about such and such?" If you looked, you would find that a good many of the books do not say anything about that question, and the ones that do, say varied things about it.

Another common name for the bible is "scripture," a term derived from the Latin *scripturae*, which simply means "writings." While it is believed to be divinely inspired, the bible is also human literature, written by historical individuals in particular cultural contexts. Because it is literature, the bible is fruitfully studied by all the methods scholars have developed for trying to understand the literary works of any culture.

The bible is divided into two major parts, the Old Testament and the New Testament, the former about three times longer than the latter. The word "testament" means covenant, a solemn agreement between two parties. Jews and Christians believe that God made a covenant of mutual faithfulness with the chosen people, the Jews, about 1200 years before Jesus of Nazareth. Christians believe that God made another covenant surpassing that one with the new chosen people, those who belong to Jesus Christ. It is Christians, therefore, who come up with the designations "Old" and "New" Testaments for the two major portions of the bible. Jews, of course, do not see their covenant with God as "old" (outmoded), nor their history with God as merely a preparation for something else. They see their history and covenant as realities possessing their own completeness and retaining permanent validity. In the dialogue among the religions today, therefore, the terms "Hebrew scriptures" and "Christian scriptures" have won acceptance as showing greater respect for both traditions. Another usage gaining favor is "First Testament" and "Second Testament." We will use the designations "Hebrew scriptures" and "Christian scriptures" here. But it should be understood that the Hebrew scriptures are in some sense also Christian scriptures, accepted by Christians too as divine revelation and part of their own bible.

There is a discrepancy among Roman Catholic, Protestant, and Jewish bibles in the number of books included in the canon of Hebrew scriptures. The "canon," a term deriving from the Greek for "measuring stick," is the official list of books regarded as inspired by God and normative for faith. A scriptural canon represents a deliberate selection from among many religious writings available, and it takes time in every religion for believers to make this selection.

There are 46 books in the Roman Catholic canon of Hebrew scriptures, while there are only 39 books in the Hebrew canon. The seven books in question are 1 and 2 Maccabees, Judith, Tobit, Baruch, Sirach, and the Wisdom of Solomon. The discrepancy came about before the Christian era, when there was still disagreement among the Jews themselves about which books among their religious writings ought to be accorded canonical status. Most of those who became Christians had, as Jews, been working with the larger collection. The Jews did not finally define their canon until around the end of the first century C.E. (Common Era). In that decision, the seven books named above were not accepted as canonical. But by this time they were well in use among Christians, and simply retained their status there.

In the Protestant reformation in the sixteenth century, Protestants opted to return to the Hebrew canon. They also reduced the number of books which had been in the canon of Christian scriptures. Martin Luther wanted to accord lesser status to Hebrews, Jude, James, and Revelation. Hence the discrepancies in books found in the various bibles today. When books not regarded as canonical are printed in a bible, they are usually grouped under the categories "apocrypha" or "deutero-canonical books."

With these points as a general introduction, we will look more closely now, first at the Hebrew scriptures, then at the Christian, to see what they contain, how they came to be written, and what sort of knowledge they offer us. Finally, we will consider some suggestions for reading the bible fruitfully.

THE HEBREW SCRIPTURES

What They Contain

The Hebrew scriptures represent a complex collection of sacred literature whose composition spans the years c. 950-150 B.C.E. (Before the Common Era; B.C.E. and C.E. are beginning to replace B.C. and A.D. as historical designations, out of respect for all those peoples who do not see history as pivoting around Jesus Christ). The period of time about which these writings speak is even longer than the period of their composition. Hebrew history starts with the patriarch Abraham, who lived about 1800 B.C.E. An even more significant figure in Hebrew history is Moses, who led the people out of Egypt and gave them the law by which they still live. These events occurred about 1200 B.C.E. This means there were several hundred years in which what is now written in the bible existed only as oral traditions, passed down from generation to generation because they were regarded as highly significant. The Hebrews were at first a nomadic people who did not employ written records to any great extent. It was only when Israel became a kingdom c. 1000 B.C.E. that the ancient traditions began to be written down in the leisure of the court. This time of writing under King David and Solomon is commonly referred to as the Golden Age of Hebrew Literature. The collection kept building over the next eight centuries as the relationship between the Hebrews and Yahweh, their God, continued to unfold. Many authors contributed, most of them nameless now.

The sacred writings have traditionally been grouped under three headings: the Law, the Prophets, and the Writings. The groupings are very rough, as the literature they comprise is quite diverse, but generally speaking "the Law" includes the Pentateuch (the first five books of the bible, regarded as especially important) and the subsequent historical books (Joshua, Judges, 1 and 2 Samuel, 1 and 2 Kings, etc.). "The Prophets" includes the three major prophets (Isaiah, Jeremiah, and Ezekiel) and the twelve minor prophets (Hosea, Joel, Amos, Micah, etc.). "The Writings" comprises all the highly variegated literature expressing the wisdom accumulated over the generations (Proverbs, Qoheleth, Job, Song of Songs, etc.). Because the Hebrews have always given more weight to the first two categories than to the third, "the Law and the Prophets" has become a kind of shorthand for the Hebrew scriptures, and the expression is used several times in the Christian gospels.

Contemporary Methods of Biblical Study

Beginning in the nineteenth century, methods of literary criticism which had originated in the renaissance and been applied fruitfully to ancient documents of various sorts began to be employed in the study of the bible. Most of those who used these methods were believers, who accepted the bible as divine revelation but were also convinced that they are documents of human literary creativity. Because the word of God in the bible comes to us in the words of humans, these scholars thought we could gain much insight into them by studying them as human literature. This would enable us to get at the mind of the authors, and understand what they were trying to say in their context rather than in ours.

The approach is called the historical critical method, and it involves several steps. First, careful attempts are made to get at the most reliable versions of the text (textual criticism). Then the text is analyzed for any materials within it which are not original, but which the author incorporated from other sources (source criticism). Then the literary forms employed in the text are analyzed (form criticism). Finally, the manner in which the authors edit or "redact" the materials at their disposal is closely watched, because it shows what their peculiar interests and convictions were (redaction criticism). The text under scrutiny is also viewed in the light of texts and other information available from the same time and place, in order to see it in its historical context. The historical critical method is in fact sometimes called "the contextual approach" because it works diligently to recover the context of the original composition.

Discoveries made through this methodology were at first threatening to believers and met with considerable resistance. Fundamentalist Christians still disown the whole approach, but it has now been accepted by most Jews and Christians as offering deeper insight into the truth while not endangering what is of the essence of faith. The conclusions it has reached enjoy the consensus of biblical scholars across most denominations.

To offer a few examples of the sort of discoveries the method has made, we now know that the book of Isaiah was not written by a single author, but by at least three authors, each with a distinct literary style, and each clearly writing in a different period. Similarly, the Psalms, traditionally attributed to David, are now recognized to be the work of many authors over several generations. The wisdom literature, traditionally ascribed to Solomon, is now seen to be an accumulation of material composed over several hundred years. It seems to have been a Hebrew literary convention to credit a whole line of literature to an illustrious figure who stood at the head of the line. Thus Moses gets credit for a good deal more law than he wrote, Solomon for more wisdom, David for more psalms. The later authors are simply anonymous.

Redaction criticism has shown us that there are two accounts of creation in the opening chapters of Genesis (ch. 1 and 2), accounts originally quite distinct but woven together so artfully as almost to sound like one account. The same is true of the story of the flood (Gen 6–9), of the betrayal of the patriarch Joseph by his brothers (Gen 37), and of many other significant events recorded throughout the bible. Different accounts or traditions existed, and were later woven into what sounds like one account until it is closely examined.

Source criticism has discovered that stories like those of creation, the fall, and the flood already existed in other religious traditions known to the Hebrews. The biblical authors used these stories because they were familiar to those for whom they were writing, but they modified them to highlight their own theological convictions.

Another discovery, of the highest importance for biblical interpretation, is that there are a rich variety of literary forms in the bible. A literary form is a standardized way of getting across an idea. Most literary forms are familiar to us from our own reading and writing. The literary form of a letter is different from the literary form of a term paper, and the literary form of a short story is different from that of an essay. The daily newspaper contains many literary forms.

There are news stories, box scores, letters to the editor, obituaries, advertisements, recipes, reviews, editorials. The difference lies not just in content but in form of presentation. The reader has to be able to distinguish literary forms if he or she wants to read the paper with understanding. An ad for a movie must be distinguished from a movie review, a news story from an editorial.

The same is true for an intelligent reading of the bible, for the bible is not all one kind of writing either. Form criticism has shown that the bible has a great many ways of trying to get across the ideas it wants to present, i.e., a rich variety of literary forms. The bible employs historical narratives, myths, homilies, poems, faith confessions, prophetic utterances, parables, laws, wise sayings, lists, prayers, proverbs, songs, and other forms. If one does not distinguish, one will read a myth as history, an edifying tale as an actual occurrence, an enthusiastic faith confession as a piece of metaphysics. Thus biblical scholars today read the Genesis accounts of creation and fall as myths, the Genesis story of the sacrifice of Isaac as a saga, the book of Jonah and the whale as a teaching tale, the account of Absalom's revolt against King David in 2 Samuel as an historical narrative. To distinguish literary forms is not to water down the sacred text, but rather to discern with care what the authors really meant to convey. This removes misunderstanding and unnecessary stumbling blocks to faith, while it unpacks the genuine riches that are there.

Two more recent developments in biblical interpretation amplify the perspectives supplied by the historical critical method. The first brings the social studies of anthropology, sociology, and psychology to bear on the writer's context—as well as on the interpreter's. The second takes a fresh direction, setting aside all historical investigation for a moment, and analyzes the text as a work of literary art crafted to speak to the reader's religious receptivity. Every writer starts with a message and a desire to get it across, and works to create a form and language most apt for successful communication. Historical criticism, while informative, can be by itself quite dry. Literary criticism invites the text to do its thing as art.

The Message of the Hebrew Scriptures

What is it that the Hebrew scriptures tell us about God and ourselves? Several themes can be crystallized. Some of them we have already seen in our consideration of images of God in the preceding chapter. God emerges as a personal being concerned with human events. The primary way in which the Hebrews come to know anything about God is through the things God does for them—liberating them from slavery in Egypt, giving them the law on Mount Sinai, leading them into the land which they come to call their own. It is with these events in mind that Moses fashions a touching portrait of God:

> The Lord your God took your part before your very eyes in Egypt as well as in the desert, where you saw how the Lord your God carried you, as a man carries his child, all along your journey until you arrived at this place (Dt 1:30-31).

The Hebrews learn to recognize God as the creator of the world and ruler of its history, awesome in power and majesty, transcendently beyond human ability to understand or even imagine. They find that this great and holy God nevertheless relates to them with tenderness, calling them as a people into a covenant relationship in which protection and guidance are extended to them in exchange for their obedience and fidelity. But they are not faithful, and this leads to another discovery about God:

Yahweh, Yahweh, a God gracious and compassionate, slow to anger, and abounding in kindness and steadfast love (Ex 34:6).

This faithful God not only gives them the law to serve as the rule of their lives, but inspires prophets to call them again and again to justice. Though many would define a prophet as one who foretells the future, the biblical prophets were actually spokespersons for God's ethical demands in times when people had gone astray. They were gadflies on the popular conscience. Their insistent message was a call to justice in human relationships and the eradication of all oppressions, and they leveled their challenge at the rich and powerful in particular. They also called people away from all idolatries—the reliance on anything less than God (riches, power, military might) for what only God can provide, human security and fulfillment. Thus even in ancient times, theology was in significant measure political. Since prophets were critics of the status quo, most of them were killed, as they are today. The link between prophets and visionaries, or those who foretell the future, is simply that the prophets told people that if they did not change their ways they would come to grief, whereas if they changed they would find peace and happiness.

This is the briefest sketch of the message of the Hebrew scriptures, but it may give some idea of the basis of the Jewish religion and the antecedents of the Christian. It should serve also to dispel the oversimplification that the God of the Hebrew scriptures is vengeful and vindictive while the God of the Christian scriptures is gracious and kind.

THE NEW TESTAMENT OR CHRISTIAN SCRIPTURES

The Christian scriptures, quite compact by comparison with the Hebrew, have been the basis of the faith of

Christians for the last two thousand years. At their center, as unifying principle, stands the figure of Jesus the Christ.

There are 27 books in the Christian scriptures, best known among them the four gospels. The rest of the books are almost all letters, though some of them use the letter form quite loosely to present treatises of Christian theology. There is also a theological history of Christian beginnings, known as the Acts of the Apostles.

The Christian scriptures were composed between the years c. 50-100 C.E., which means that the earliest writing commenced some 20 years after the death/resurrection of Jesus, and went on for about two generations. The present order of placement in the bible does not reflect the order of composition. The letters of Paul are the earliest writings, composed during the 50s. The gospels come next, Mark the first, John the last. The rest of the letters fill out the last decades of the first century, some of them possibly composed early in the second century.

The same methods of historical critical analysis applied to the Hebrew scriptures have been applied fruitfully to the Christian, yielding the knowledge we now have about dates of composition, literary forms, and the developing interpretation of Jesus among the first Christians.

Because the gospels are the most important Christian literature, let us examine them first. Then we will look at the letters of Paul, and the rest of the writings.

The Synoptic Gospels

The first three gospels show a strong resemblance to one another, whereas the gospel of John has a character all its own. For this reason, the first three are called "the synoptic gospels." The term means that they can be lined up in parallel columns, as they often are for study, and surveyed in a single glance. This is so because they recount, with minor variations, so many of the same incidents and teachings, and in much the same order.

The process by which the gospels came to be composed is particularly interesting. At first nothing was written down. Many early Christians believed that the end of the world would come in their lifetime, and Jesus would return in glory. His words and deeds were passed on orally from the original eyewitnesses to those who were brought into the faith. As these traditions were used in instructing converts, in preaching, and in the eucharist, they acquired standard literary form as isolated units—miracle stories, parables of Jesus, stories about Jesus, blocks of teaching, pronouncement stories (i.e., controversial situations ending with famous one-liners of Jesus, e.g., "The sabbath is made for people, not people for the sabbath"). As the end of the world was delayed and the community kept growing, and as the original eyewitnesses began to die off, the need was felt to write down these cherished traditions. Mark's gospel was the first surviving attempt to do that. It was written about 65, with Matthew and Luke following about 80-85, and John about 90 C.E. Each gospel was composed in a different city, for the Christians of a major community.

Mark took the oral traditions of his acquaintance and arranged them into a continuous narrative from the beginning of the public life of Jesus through his death and resurrection. Literary analysis has shown how skillfully he performed his task, with clear theological convictions governing the project. Writing for a community that was suffering persecution, Mark portrays a Jesus who suffers opposition from early in his ministry, begins to predict his crucifixion in Jerusalem, and embraces his fate with courage and hope when it comes. Mark is the shortest of the gospels, giving us relatively little of the teaching of Jesus, concentrating more on narrating the main events. In his narratives, Mark includes more details than the others do. Unique to Mark are four memorable snapshots of Jesus: Jesus sound asleep in a boat on a cushion (4:38), Jesus looking upon the rich young man with love (10:17), Jesus taking children into his arms (10:13), and Jesus walking on ahead of his fearful disciples to Jerusalem where he would suffer (10:32).

Mark's gospel shows a clear turning point at 8:27, where Peter recognizes Jesus as the messiah or Christ, i.e., as the one anointed by God and sent as savior. Up to this point, Jesus deals with the crowds in a series of miracles and controversies. After it, Jesus concentrates on the disciples, instructing them privately in the central Christian mystery of death and resurrection. Then comes the final confrontation with the authorities in Jerusalem, bringing on Jesus' death.

When Matthew and Luke wrote their gospels about twenty years later, both had Mark before them. They took over 90% of Mark's material, and generally followed Mark's order of presentation, using his gospel as a framework. But they edited Mark's material in various ways, and into his structure they inserted large blocks of Jesus' teaching. They took this material from another written document they had, a document scholars named "Q," the first letter of the German word *Quelle*, which means "source." We no longer possess this collection of Jesus' teachings. The reason scholars posit a written source rather than oral tradition for this material is that Matthew and Luke render it practically word for word the same and usually in the same sequence of teachings, strongly suggesting a written document.

Besides Mark and Q as common written sources, Matthew and Luke each had another source peculiar to himself, as each gospel contains material the other lacks and Mark does not have either. Thus Matthew alone has, for example, the story of the magi at Jesus' birth, the parable of the merciless debtor, the parable of the wise and foolish virgins, and the last judgment scene. Luke alone has, for example, the annunciation to Mary, the story of the prostitute who washes Jesus' feet, the parable of the prodigal son, and the story of Jesus and Herod during the passion.

Like Mark, each of these gospels has its distinctive character. Matthew writes for a community of Jews turned Christians. So he portrays Jesus as a great teacher, like Moses. He even divides his gospel into five "books," resembling Moses' Pentateuch. His genealogy traces Jesus back to Abraham, the father of the Jews. At every point, he is at pains to show how Jesus fulfills the Hebrew scriptures, quoting those scriptures some 41 times. He wants to prove that Jesus is the expected messiah or Christ, and that the Christian community is the new Israel.

Luke's is a more universal gospel. He writes not for Jewish but for Gentile converts. His genealogy therefore traces Jesus back to Adam, the father of the human race. He makes fewer references to the Hebrew scriptures, and presents Jesus to the Gentiles not so much as teacher, but as prophet, i.e., as one sent by God to make the divine will known in word and action.

Luke's is preeminently the gospel of sinners. In addition to the parable of the prodigal son and the washing of Jesus' feet by a prostitute, Luke alone gives us the parables of the lost sheep and the lost coin, Jesus in the home of the despised tax collector Zacchaeus, Jesus' pardon of his executioners and of the thief crucified with him, and Jesus' statement "Be merciful as your heavenly Father is merciful" (where Matthew has instead, "Be perfect as your heavenly Father is perfect").

Luke's is preeminently the gospel of the poor and lowly. It opens with the story of the childless couple Zechariah and Elizabeth, then presents the humble Mary and Joseph. It

describes the visit of shepherds to Jesus' birthplace (Matthew
has magi), and recounts the story of the old man Simeon and
the elderly widow Anna in the temple at Jesus' presentation.
More than any other gospel, Luke emphasizes the need to
give up riches to follow Jesus. Luke stands out among the synoptics as the gospel of women, themselves lowly in Jesus' culture but prominent in his company. Besides the ones already
named, there are his friends Martha and Mary, and the group
of women who travel with him ministering to his needs. Luke
also lays great emphasis on the work of the Holy Spirit, a
theme which continues in his other contribution to the
Christian scriptures, the Acts of the Apostles.

The Gospel of John

John writes last, about 90 C.E., and his is a fresh
approach to gospel writing. He chooses just a handful of the
stories available from the miracle tradition, names each a
sign rather than a work of power in order to call attention to
the deeper meaning in it, and follows the action with a
lengthy discourse of Jesus elaborating its significance. An
example is the multiplication of the loaves and the long
discourse following it about Jesus as the bread of life, which
occupy all of chapter 6; or the healing of the blind man and
the long discourse following it about Jesus as the light of the
world, which occupy all of chapter 9. John has no stories
about Jesus' infancy (neither does Mark), but gives us a
brilliant prologue instead, a hymn celebrating the word of
God become human flesh. John has no baptism of Jesus and
no temptations in the desert. He has no transfiguration, nor
the synoptics' three predictions of the passion. He has no
institution of the eucharist, and no agony in the garden. In
fact, John has only about 8% of the synoptic material. The
rest is his own. Instead of the institution of the eucharist at

the last supper, he gives us Jesus washing the disciples' feet. Where the last supper is only a part of one chapter in each of the synoptics, John has a supper lasting for five chapters, as Jesus discourses at length with his intimates.

John's portrait of the person of Jesus is distinctive too. John heavily accents the divine dimension, portraying a Jesus who is from above, eternal, knowing what is in people's hearts and what is to come, and making for himself very exalted claims:

> Before Abraham was, I am (8:58).
> I am the bread of life (6:48).
> I am the way, the truth, and the life (14:6).
> I am the light of the world (9:5).
> The Father and I are one (10:30).

This presentation of Jesus' divinity, while it is not a complete departure from the synoptic rendition, does represent a considerable development, and marks John's interpretation of Jesus as distinctive.

Reflections on the Gospels

As can now be seen, the four gospels are a very special kind of literature. The evangelists (the term means bringer of good news) are not detached secular historians. They do not write either history or biography as people do today, with video cameras present at the actual events, using interviews with the principal subject and significant intimates, trying to get at inner consciousness as well as outer event. The evangelists are all believers and enthusiasts, writing at a distance of 30-60 years from the career of Jesus, motivated by a desire to share the new life they have found in him. They want to tell the story of his ministry, but they also want to tell of the immense transformation which took place in him with his resurrection from the dead so that he still lives and is open to a living relationship with anyone who seeks it. Their dilemma is how best to present all this.

Who the four final editors of this sacred tradition are, we do not know. We do know that they have at their disposal both oral and written materials which go back to eyewitnesses. These traditions have already undergone considerable transformation as they are used in many localities and situations for instruction, exhortation, and liturgical celebration. Christians have lived through a generation or two of trying to be disciples of Jesus in interaction with surrounding cultures. They have encountered new problems and questions, and gained new insights along the way. Now the evangelists are writing for yet other communities with their own challenges and dilemmas.

All of this feeds into their work, governing their selection of incidents and teachings and their editing of these materials that they might speak with maximal clarity and effect to the needs of the developing church. The resurrection, with all that it makes clear about Jesus, affects the way they present his whole life. They superimpose their present insights back onto the public ministry, feeling free even to put words into the mouth of Jesus, the better to express his full significance for them. This freedom is greatest in the fourth gospel. The gospels, then, are confessional documents, calculated primarily not to narrate history, though they rest on an historical bedrock, but to arouse and sustain the life of Christian faith. The same could undoubtedly be said, with variations, of the Hebrew scriptures, the Buddhist scriptures, and the ancient scriptures of the other great traditions. New Testament scholars today expend much energy trying to distinguish authentic sayings of the historical Jesus from sayings ascribed to him over the next two to three generations of gospel evolution.

The Letters of Paul

After the gospels, the documents most influential in shaping Christian understanding are the letters of Paul. The letters we are sure come from Paul were written during the 50s: 1 Thessalonians, Galatians, Philippians, Philemon, 1 and 2 Corinthians, and Romans. On the basis chiefly of stylistic differences, many scholars doubt that 2 Thessalonians, Colossians, Ephesians, 1 and 2 Timothy, and Titus come from Paul, though they might well come from disciples of his. Even further removed from Paul's style and dominant conceptions is the letter to the Hebrews. That these later letters have traditionally been attributed to Paul follows a principle enunciated earlier. In the bible generally, later literature is ascribed to the great forerunners.

Paul represents a distinctive and invaluable point of view. He was not one of the original followers of Jesus. He was a very serious Jew who saw the Jesus movement as false to the tradition and pernicious, and he zealously persecuted the church. We can imagine his surprise when he had an overpowering experience of the risen Jesus as he was traveling to Damascus to round up some more Christians for prosecution. The encounter, recounted in Acts 9, made a believer out of him, and furnished him with the two key convictions of his theology: Jesus is Lord, and the church is his body. We have in Paul a key witness to Jesus' resurrection, as he was a person not the least predisposed to believe in it.

Paul understood himself as called to be an apostle to the Gentiles, in contrast to Peter whose call was to his fellow Jews. The peculiar way in which Paul came into relation with the Christian movement is reflected in his writings. He never speaks of Jesus' public life or refers back to any of his teachings or powerful works. His whole focus is on Jesus' death and resurrection and their significance for humanity. Where others accent Jesus' sublime teachings and the beauty of his example, Paul's exclusive focus is on how Jesus accepted a painful and humiliating death for others, on how God exalted him as a consequence, on how Jesus lives now in those who belong to him (the church), and on how all who believe in him will themselves be raised from death to everlasting life.

For all the brilliance of his theological insight, Paul is many Christians' least favorite writer. This is partly because he speaks in terms quite foreign to us and is difficult to understand, particularly in the short snippets from his letters which are read at Sunday liturgies. It is also because some of his work reflects a cultural sexism unpalatable to large numbers of women and men today. A man of his time, Paul likewise accepts the institution of slavery and without qualification enjoins obedience to civil governments as authorized by God. Christian conscience has since moved beyond these positions. It is also Paul, not Jesus, who argues for celibacy as the highest form of Christian existence. At work here might well have been his conviction that the end of the world was coming any minute, and there were more urgent things to do than marry and start families.

Yet, for all his limitations, Paul has left Christians countless passages of profound insight and enormous power. It is Paul who edited and promulgated the great hymn celebrating the primacy of love over all other religious manifestations (1 Cor 13), the brilliant discussion of wisdom and foolishness, power and weakness in God and human beings (1 Cor 1-4), the ingenious development of the body metaphor to describe the Christian community's interrelatedness and incorporation into Christ (Rom 12, 1 Cor 12). It is Paul who left us such memorable one-liners as:

For me, to live is Christ, and to die is gain (Phil 1:21).

He loved me, and delivered himself up for me (Gal 2:20).

If God is for us, who can be against us (Rom 8:31)?

I can do all things in him who strengthens me (Phil 4:13).

For those who love God, God makes all things work together for good (Rom 8:28).

I live, now not I, but Christ lives in me (Gal 2:20).

Other Early Christian Writings

Besides the letters of Paul, the Christian scriptures include letters ascribed to John, James, Peter, and Jude, epistles called "catholic" because they are addressed *universally* (the root meaning of "catholic") rather than to a *particular* congregation as Paul's letters were. The letters of John contain many of the same themes as the fourth gospel, and are held to come from the same school of thought, if not from the same individual. The other letters, written late in the first or early in the second century, are almost certainly not written by the apostles to whom they are ascribed. But they are accepted as inspired and as part of the canon.

The Acts of the Apostles is a theological history of the beginnings of the church, starting in Jerusalem with Jesus' ascension and the descent of the Holy Spirit, and ending in Rome, the capital of the world, where Paul seeds the gospel prior to his martyrdom. Written by Luke, it contains sketches of some of the earliest Christian preaching, accounts of typical Christian struggles, and the story of the rapid spread of the faith beyond the Jews into the Gentile world.

The letter to the Hebrews is a reflection on the significance of Jesus from the viewpoint of an unknown Jewish Christian with marked priestly interests.

The book of Revelation, also known as the Apocalypse

(the Greek word means "uncovering" or "revelation"), comes under that genre of biblical literature known as apocalyptic, of which we have other examples in the books of Zechariah, Joel, and Daniel. This type of literature is always proposed under the name of some celebrity (John, in this case), and presents a vision of future events. It uses symbolic communication extensively and speaks of a cataclysmic end of the world after a bitter struggle between the forces of good and evil. The author of Revelation calls himself John (Rev 1:1). Every literary indication is that he is not the person who wrote John's gospel. The work's symbolic language is very difficult to interpret, and perhaps for this very reason has attracted countless aspiring interpreters. Almost every age in the Christian era has seen itself in this book and expected an imminent end of the world, a fact which ought to introduce some sobriety into the assessment of the many contemporaneous inter- pretations of this ancient document. Some fine biblical scholarship in recent years makes the original intent of Revelation available to us. It was a letter written to sustain Christians in the midst of trial and persecution, and as such it retains perennial value. We will say more about this in the chapter on the end of the world.

Besides the 27 books which comprise the Christian scriptures, many other books were written in the wake of the Jesus event—other gospels, epistles, apocalypses, etc. These did not make it into the Christian canon, but some of them have survived and are available in libraries. They shed helpful light on early Christian thought and life. Decisions about which books to canonize evolved only gradually over many generations of Christian experience. It was not until the end of the fourth century that the canon was fixed.

The Question of Inspiration and Inerrancy

~~All Christians believe the bible is the word of God, inspired by the Holy Spirit.~~ But this admits of various understandings among the denominations, and sometimes even within them. ~~Fundamentalist Christians understand it to mean that the bible is literally God's own communication,~~ dictated by God as it stands. Because of this, ~~it can contain no error, even of history or science.~~ Thus any biblical verse can be quoted as God's own pronouncement upon a given issue.

The mainline Roman Catholic and Protestant churches share with fundamentalists a belief in the divine inspiration of the bible, but they do not understand this to mean that the words of the bible are God's own words. They accept the historical and literary findings of scholars, and so are aware of the human dimension of all the sacred books as well. Thus they view inspiration as a more complex phenomenon, as a kind of synergy, or working together, of the divine and the human, such that it is God who communicates in the bible but always through the limitations of a culturally situated human being. This human mediator of divine communication is assisted by God's inspiration, but never in such a way as to escape the human condition. Thus, the biblical writer composes not only within the culturally specific horizons of a given time and place, but also within the inescapable human limitation against ever being able to express the transcendent mystery of God's being, action, or will in a fully adequate way.

Also, in this more generally accepted understanding of inspiration, it is the *whole* bible that is inspired. Insight and understanding evolve within the bible itself as experience and reflection accumulate. and the writings, spanning more than a thousand years, must be interpreted as a whole.

For example, the early biblical idea that God wants believers to destroy entire nations of unbelievers gives way later in the bible to greater respect and tolerance for other peoples. The early idea that God is angry and vengeful and strikes at once to punish wrongdoing gives way to the later insight that God is gracious and kind and slow to anger. The early idea that if you obey God's law you will prosper but if you disobey you will encounter disaster, gives way on the basis of more experience to bafflement over the prosperity of the wicked and the suffering of the good.

Christians who read the bible with sensitivity to its human historical evolution avoid quoting isolated verses which sound as if God clearly stands for capital punishment, against homosexuality, for white supremacy, for slavery, for genocide, for polygamy, for male dominance. Careful readers always take into account the historical context of a given utterance, to understand what the issue was, what the cultural assumptions were, what the language used meant then, and what the whole thing might mean in our present situation. They allow diverse passages to correct one another. Finally, they try to understand how the bible taken as a whole sheds light on any given passage within it.

SOME SUGGESTIONS FOR READING THE BIBLE

The only way really to come to know the bible is to read it. No overview or introduction can begin to substitute for that. Perhaps we could round out our treatment with some thoughts on how to approach the bible as an interested reader—a believer or one who might like to be.

Such a person opens the book expecting to encounter the living God in it. The desire for a word of instruction, illumination, inspiration for one's life takes precedence over all other considerations. So one opens not only the book but heart and mind as well, perhaps even starting with a prayer that God's word might be deeply heard, understood, and assimilated.

1) *Read it as a living word.* Much of the biblical material deals with events that transpired long ago. Yet the bible is a living word, addressed by the God who lives to the believer of any age who is attuned to hear God speak. The events that are recorded are there because they are paradigmatic, i.e., they are typical frames for the encounter between God and human beings. Thus when, in Exodus, I read of God's people leaving their bondage in Egypt, I am reading of what God is doing with me right now or wants to do for me, leading me out of whatever bondage I may be in. When I read of the call that Judith or Jeremiah received from God, I open myself to hear what God's call to me might be right now. When I read of Jesus moved with compassion and laying his hand on a leper, I am reading of what I need myself and what Jesus could do for me now if I want him to. I am also reading of how I need to be moved with compassion at the suffering around me and take action to alleviate it. The bible thus serves as a medium for God's present communication and action. Whenever it is read privately or proclaimed publicly, the word of God comes to life again.

2) *Use your imagination.* Enter into the text and live it as if it were your own story. When we listen to someone tell a story, we instinctively identify with one of the characters, sometimes with more than one. The bible offers us many characters to identify with. In the gospel story of Jesus' passion, for instance, we can identify with Pilate washing his hands of the whole business, the women weeping at the wayside as they watch this beloved man being brutally destroyed, Peter suddenly terrified and denying that he and Jesus ever had anything to do with one another, Jesus himself carrying the cross to Golgotha. Each of these identifications is illuminating. The best way to experience the force of Jesus' parables is actually to become, imaginatively, the person who has been mugged in the parable of the good Samaritan (Lk

10), or the person who helps. Become the father who welcomes back the son who has grieved him in the parable of the prodigal son (Lk 15), or the brother who does not appreciate this generosity at all. Be the mother hen who tries to gather her unwilling chicks under her wings (Lk 13), or a chick who is resistant. There is still another way to catch the force of a passage as if for the first time. Most of Jesus' listeners were poor people living under oppression. Be an oppressed person in his audience or in contemporary society, and hear the word as a poor person would hear it. The bible is written to challenge and change us. We give it the power only when we get beyond being mere analysts, and enter into the text.

3) *Read the bible in the believing community.* Reading along with other people helps. There is not only the greater richness of sharing many different experiences of the word, but also the corrective supplied by other people to one's own possible exaggerations and misunderstandings. Other believers can be present not only in person but also in the form of books of introduction and commentary, bringing the findings of biblical scholarship and the fruits of prayerful reflection to the reader. In the worshiping assembly, many together hear the word proclaimed and preached upon by those who have made a closer study of it. These communal sharings nourish one's private use of the bible for reading and prayer.

Authoritative and important as the bible is, it is not the whole universe of religious experience. It is seen most truly when viewed within a context larger than itself, the whole universe of human experience from which it was itself derived. A traditional story illustrates this point.

> One day a man entered a remote mountain village and asked for asylum there. In the course of a few weeks' stay, the villagers became impressed with his goodness, without being able to find out why he had come.

Then a military general with numerous troops came to the village. "We know you are hiding a traitor here," he said. "If you do not hand him over to us, we will destroy your entire village."

Days of debate in the town council led to no conclusion. So the mayor took the matter up with the priest. The two spent a whole night searching the scriptures and finally came up with a solution. There was a text that said, "It is better that one man die and the nation be saved."

So the mayor handed over the innocent man to the general, begging the man's pardon. The man said there was nothing to pardon. He did not want to put the village in jeopardy. He was tortured cruelly and put to death.

Some years later a prophet came to the village. He asked for the mayor and said to him, "What did you do? That man was appointed by God to be the savior of this country, and you gave him up to torture and execution!"

"What could I do?" pleaded the mayor. "The priest and I searched the scriptures, and acted accordingly."

"That was your mistake," said the prophet sadly. "You looked at the scriptures. You should also have looked into the man's eyes."

SUMMARY

The bible has had tremendous impact on human civilization, and has foundational importance for two of the world's great religions. The Hebrew scriptures, its first part, record some 1800 years of the religious experience of the Hebrews. The Christian scriptures, its second part, record the life, death, and resurrection of Jesus of Nazareth and the beginnings of the church which bears his name. The bible is regarded by Jewish and Christian believers alike as inspired by God and giving us authentic revelation.

At the same time, believers have always recognized the human dimension of all we find in the bible. Biblical scholarship today is particularly aware of the cultural contexts in which the bible was composed and the literary forms it employs to express religious truth. Meanwhile theology keeps us reminded of the inability of human beings ever adequately to express the mystery of God. In this chapter we have looked at how the bible came to be, what sorts of materials it contains, and how to read it intelligently and fruitfully.

Questions and Exercises

1. What do the following terms mean: bible, scripture, canon, Old Testament, New Testament, apocrypha, synoptic, apocalyptic?

2. How old are the Hebrew and Christian scriptures? What period of time does each cover? Why was there some delay in each case before anything was written down?

3. Why are there discrepancies in what the Jewish, Roman Catholic, and Protestant bibles contain?

4. What is the historical critical method of biblical study? What light has it shed on our understanding of scripture? What is literary criticism?

5. What are some of the major theological themes of the Hebrew scriptures?

6. How did the gospels come to be composed? How are the first three gospels interrelated?

7. What are some of the distinctive characteristics of each of the gospels?

8. Why is Paul such an important Christian figure? What are some of his distinctive theological themes?

9. What does it mean to say the bible is inspired?

10. How should one approach the bible to derive spiritual profit from it?

11. Read through the first eleven chapters of Genesis, and see if you can spot the weaving together of different versions of the same story.

12. Locate a book which presents the synoptic gospels in parallel columns, and compare the different versions of the same incidents or teachings.

13. Take a parable of Jesus and enter it imaginatively, becoming now one, now another, of its characters, letting your imagination go beyond the interaction given in the text. How do you find the experience?

Suggestions for Further Reading

Dianne Bergant and Robert Karris, eds., *The Collegeville Bible Commentary*, 2 vols. (Liturgical Press, 1992). Roman Catholic biblical scholars offer concise overviews and commentaries on each biblical book, with sensitivity to contemporary concerns such as feminism and interfaith dialogue.

Raymond Brown, *Responses to 101 Questions on the Bible* (Paulist, 1990). A leading Roman Catholic scholar answers common questions asked about the bible and Christian faith in light of recent scholarship.

Anthony Ceresko, *Introduction to the Old Testament: A Liberation Perspective* (Orbis, 1992). Brings the perspective of liberation theology to the reading of the Hebrew scriptures.

Carol Newsom and Sharon Ringe, eds., *The Women's Bible Commentary* (Westminster, 1992). Women biblical scholars offer an introduction to each book of the bible with a commentary on those sections of each book which have particular relevance to women.

Pheme Perkins, *Reading the New Testament: An Introduction* (Paulist, 1988). A basic introduction to the Christian scriptures.

Sandra Schneiders, *The Revelatory Text: Interpreting the New Testament as Sacred Scripture* (HarperSanFrancisco, 1991). A clear exposition of current exegetical method put at the service of scripture as Word meant to nourish the spiritual life.

John Spong, *Rescuing the Bible from Fundamentalism: A Bishop Rethinks the Meaning of Scripture* (HarperSanFrancisco, 1992). An Episcopal bishop uses modern scholarship to show the inadequacies and dangers of a fundamentalist reading of the bible.

CHAPTER 5

Jesus

About two thousand years ago a man lived in Palestine whose career has had immense impact on the world. He was an itinerant Jewish rabbi by the name of Yeshua—Jesus, in English. He is often called Christ, but in this chapter we will call him Jesus, because Jesus was his given name whereas Christ was a title applied to him later.

Living in a very religious milieu, Jesus articulated a religious vision significantly different from that of most of his contemporaries. He won an enthusiastic following and aroused bitter opposition at the same time. By those who loved him, Jesus was remembered for his simple but provocative stories and for all the good he did as he moved among the sick, the guilty, the alienated, and the powerful. His love was large enough to embrace everyone, and he had a gift for healing. He gravitated by preference toward the lower classes, with whom he frequently ate and drank. His intimates were fishermen and a group of women who traveled with them on their journeys providing for their material needs (Lk 8:1-3).

The central theme of Jesus' preaching was the reign of God, which he was convinced was coming in a new and powerful way, and he enunciated God's requirements for being part of that reign, issuing a call to a profound change of heart. The Jewish leaders of the time turned him over to the

Roman authorities who ruled the country, and Jesus was executed on political charges. He was crucified with the contemptuous inscription "Jesus of Nazareth, King of the Jews" over his head. His followers laid him to rest in the tomb of a wealthy friend.

A few days later an amazing thing happened. He was seen alive by many witnesses, individually and in groups, people who had known him and grieved his passing. These appearances continued for some time. Those who saw Jesus bore witness that God had raised him from the dead and glorified him, and that his message was to be preached to the ends of the earth. This was the beginning of the community of Christians called church, and of its missionary movement. Both have had a major impact on human history.

In the gospels and other books of the Christian scriptures, there is considerable reflection on who this Jesus is. Because of his manifest goodness, his powers of healing, the patent truth of his utterances, his familiarity with God, and his resurrection from death, Jesus attracts to himself practically every title of honor and divinity that exists in the Hebrew, Greek, and Roman world of his time. He is called just one, holy one, servant of God, Christ (the term means a person anointed by God for a special task), master, prophet, messiah (same as Christ, Aramaic instead of Greek), savior, lord, rabbi (teacher), son of David (the greatest of Hebrew kings), son of God, son of man, word of God, and others, some fifty of them in all in the Christian scriptures. In a few places in scripture, Jesus is even called God (Jn 1:1-14; Jn 20:28). His followers thus bequeath a variety of names, reflecting a variety of conceptions of the richness of his person and work.

Speculation continues through the next couple of centuries, in a milieu increasingly dominated by Greek rather than Hebrew ways of thinking. At a council of the church held at Nicaea in 325, Jesus is said to be "one in being with the Father," or "one in substance with the Father." At another council, held in Chalcedon in 451, Jesus is pronounced "true God and true man." These definitions, strongly influenced by Greek philosophical modes of analysis, become normative for the church's faith.

It is clear from the Christian scriptures that a person's lived response to the challenge and invitation of Jesus is far more important than any specific confession concerning his identity. Let us look then at how Jesus functions in the lived experience of those committed to him. Then let us make a closer examination of his life and teaching, his death, and his resurrection, to uncover their implications.

JESUS IN THE LIVES OF CHRISTIANS

What is Jesus in the lived experience of those who believe in him? He is the object of love, emulation, and worship. We venerate representations of him in paintings, statues, crucifixes. We pray to him and worship him, whether as God or as the holy human mediator between ourselves and God, the one who, in the metaphoric language of Ephesians, "sits at the right hand of the Father" (Eph 1:20). We celebrate the eucharist together, commemorating the last supper Jesus shared with his disciples, and in this symbolic reenactment of his death and resurrection, we believe we enjoy communion with him now. Even aside from eucharistic communion, we believe Jesus abides in us through his Spirit.

We see in Jesus the symbol of God's love, and in his suffering and death God's involvement in human grief and pain. Heeding Jesus' call, we labor with him to further God's reign in the world. We strive to base our lives on his teachings and example, seeing in him the full flower of our own best possibilities. Thus, what Jesus is for us as Christians is both the fullest expression of divinity and the highest realization of humanity. Hans Küng, surveying the world religious scene and asking what is unique to Christianity among the religions, answers that it is Jesus. The observation may seem obvious, but it hits the center. Christian life is built entirely around this person Jesus.

JESUS' LIFE AND TEACHING

If Jesus' life and teaching are the norm for Christian living, what are their main features?

1) *Jesus lives with and for God.* Perhaps the most unmistakable feature of the life of Jesus is the centrality and depth of his relationship with God. It shows in many ways. He prays much. We find him at prayer not only at critical junctures in his life, but whenever he can get away from the crowds of a morning or evening (Mk 1:35). He speaks familiarly of God in parables and other teaching, as if he knows exactly how God sees things and what God wants of us. So assured is his teaching about God that people remark: "He teaches as one having authority, and not as the scribes and Pharisees" (Mt 7:29). Jesus conducts himself as a person with a mission, seeking always to do the will of the one who sent him, striving to accomplish God's work (Jn 4:34). He frequently refers to God as "my Father," not just as "our Father" (Jn 20:17), and goes further still, calling God "Abba," as we have seen. In this God he puts his entire trust, in life and in death.

Uniquely intimate as Jesus' relationship with God is, he describes that God as gracious to *all*, as wanting to relate in love with each of us. Jesus teaches that we are all God's children, that God has numbered the hairs of our heads, that God will give us what we ask for, that in fact God knows what we need before we ask, and that God will take care of our needs if we seek to do what is right (Mt 6:33). Jesus teaches that we show our love for God by doing God's will (Mt 7:21). Yet, in his parables as well as in his own ministry, Jesus shows God's readiness to forgive us our failings and continue to be faithful to us in spite of them (Lk 15).

2) *Jesus lives his life in the service of others.* Open the gospel to any page, and you will find Jesus doing something for someone. He is forgiving sins, healing diseases, freeing people from what limits them, feeding a crowd, calming a storm, teaching or answering questions, inviting or encouraging someone. He boldly confronts religious and political leaders, this too in the interest of suffering people (e.g., Mt 23). Jesus' outstanding human quality is his concern. He feels others' pain and devotes himself to easing it (Mt 9:36). Indeed his dedication to God seems to consist chiefly in this total commitment to the well-being of the human community.

There is something remarkable about the scope of his love. Most people love someone. It seems that Jesus had a heart large enough to embrace everyone. Though he was sought out by at least some of the rich and powerful of his day, his preference was for those at the bottom of the social ladder. He ate with prostitutes and other "sinners" with sufficient regularity to get the reputation of being "a glutton and a drunkard" (Mt 11:19). He showed interest in and appreciation of women in a culture in which men looked down on women. He allowed himself to be accosted in public by blind people, deaf people, lepers and cripples. Thus, in religious terms, Jesus was neither an ascetic nor a hermit. Rather, he was a person in the midst of others, helping them as best he could with the difficulties of life. He succeeded in reviving people's faith in themselves and moving them to relate to others along the lines he did.

Jesus calls us to follow him. He urges us to share our goods with others (Mk 10), to help the person who has fallen victim at the side of the road (Lk 10), to feed the hungry and visit the prisoner (Mt 25). He asks us to forgive those who have injured us, and to do it over and over (Mt 18). He encourages us to love not just our friends but our enemies as well—those who hate us, speak ill of us, persecute us—and to do good to them (Lk 6:27). He asks us to serve one another even to washing one another's feet (Jn 13), and to seek the lowest place rather than the highest (Lk 14). In Jesus' view, it is not enough to love just family and friends, or even just those of our own nation or religion. His vision of community takes in all humanity. He seeks to break down all barriers that stand between "us" and "them," to reconcile all human beings with God and one another.

The teaching of Jesus is brought to focus in his own simple summary of it, given in Jerusalem near the end of his public life. In answer to a question which commandment is the greatest, he says:

> "The first is, 'Hear, O Israel, the Lord our God is one God, and you must love the Lord your God with your whole heart and with your whole soul and with your whole mind and with your whole strength.' The second is this, 'You must love your neighbor as yourself'" (Mk 12:30-31. Jesus is quoting Dt 6:4-6 and Lv 19:18.)

The religious genius of Jesus consists precisely in the intertwining of the two parts of this one commandment. One's relationships with fellow human beings are thus made the heart of one's religion. When John and Paul comment on the love commandment, they too make love of neighbor the essential expression of one's commitment to God.

> If any make the statement: "I love God," and yet hate a brother or sister, they lie. For those who do not love their brothers and sisters, whom they have seen, cannot be loving God, whom they have not seen (1 Jn 4:20).

> Those who love their fellow men and women have
> fulfilled the law (Rom 13:8).

> Bear one another's burdens, and so fulfill the law of
> Christ (Gal 6:2).

There is another major emphasis in the teaching of
Jesus, and it flows from the great commandment. In many
different ways, Jesus enjoins the renunciation of riches. He
tells us not to lay up treasure for ourselves on earth (Mt 6). He
calls the poor blessed, and pronounces woes on the rich (Lk
6). In a typical encounter, he tells a rich young man he should
sell all he has and give to the poor, and come and follow him
(Mk 10). He says it is easier for a camel to get through the eye
of a needle than for a rich person to enter God's kingdom
(Mk 10). In a parable, he describes a man who is busy building himself bigger barns, and calls him a fool (Lk 12). His
parable of the rich man and the beggar at his gate ends with
the beggar in the bosom of Abraham and the rich man in
Hades (Lk 16). One out of every ten verses in the synoptics is
about riches and poverty, one out of seven in Luke.

The way this theme in Jesus' teaching flows from the
overarching commandment is, first, as he says himself, we
cannot serve both God and mammon. They involve conflicting sets of values. Second, there are so many needy people
around us that we can hardly say we love them when we are
busy building ourselves an economic empire and walling
them out.

The cultural situation in which we live today is far more
complex than the cultural situation Jesus lived in. Those
who draw out the implications of Jesus' teaching about
riches and poverty for the present context call our attention
to the way we place our security today in our riches and
armaments rather than in God. We idolize our comfortable
way of life and the nuclear warheads that hedge it about. If

we really sought to live under God's reign we would adopt quite different ways. The small percentage of wealthy people in the world today (the U.S., for instance, has about 5% of the world's population) live at the expense of the vast poor majority. If we were really to love the people of Latin America, the people of Asia, the people of Africa, we would have to change our way of life. It would not be enough to give them a little foreign aid to feed their starving. We would have to change the very structure of the world economy to correct the immense imbalances which imprison the great majority in misery for the benefit of the few.

Such considerations may seem a long way from the simple teaching of Jesus. But we catch the significance of Jesus' vision and purpose only if we see it in terms of our own situation. Loving God and loving neighbor can sound so easy that people think they are already doing it if they love their best friends and have vaguely benevolent feelings toward the rest of humanity. What Jesus calls us to is far broader, deeper, and more difficult.

Before we leave the teaching of Jesus, we might make reference to one item absent from our summary. That is sex. The reason sex is not here is that it is at best a minor key in the life and teaching of Jesus. This seems worth remarking because so often when the Christian life is presented, sexual prohibitions are a very prominent part of the presentation. Indeed, the image of the Christian church in many minds is that of an institution negatively preoccupied with sex—no masturbation, no homosexuality, no extramarital sex, no "impure thoughts" even. The Roman Catholic Church goes further, making much of the issue of birth control, and insisting on celibacy for all its clergy.

If Jesus had shown a negative attitude toward sexuality and made sex a prominent issue in his teaching, the posture of the church would be understandable. But that is the anomaly. Sex is a subject on which Jesus says very little. There is nothing in the gospels on masturbation, homosexuality, premarital sex, or birth control. Jesus does speak against adultery, but adultery involves a serious breach of marital covenant. Jesus speaks against lust, but this teaching takes up only one verse and is found in only one of the gospels (Mt 5:28). Nowhere in the New Testament are we told Jesus was celibate, but if he was he makes no point of it, and the men in his inner circle of disciples are all married (with the possible exception of John). When he deals with anyone who has gone wrong sexually, he simply forgives the person, no questions asked. The gospels hardly constitute a basis for the church's preoccupation with sexual issues. Paul's letters lie at the root of some of it, along with dualistic (spirit vs. body) non-Christian cultural currents which found their way early into Christian theology.

This is not to say sexuality is not an important moral issue. It is, obviously. Sexual exploitation hurts people. Integrating our sexual energy into authentic and responsible loving is for everyone a personal task at once crucial and sufficiently challenging to last a lifetime. If learning to love is the highest value in the Christian life, then learning to integrate our sexuality into genuine loving is a matter of the greatest importance. What Jesus gives us is the *norm* for the expression of our sexuality, not a detailed sexual ethic. And it is unmistakable that he talks a great deal more about the economic implications of the love commandment than he does about the sexual implications. The churches, for whatever reasons, have reversed the proportions.

JESUS' DEATH

It should not surprise us that Jesus did not live to be very old. The end came violently. It has sometimes been said that this violent end was the whole purpose of his existence, that "he came down to die." This is far too simple. Jesus' death cannot be detached from his life, especially when the gospels are so careful to preserve his life story and narrate the conflicts that led to his execution. It was precisely the things Jesus said and did that turned the authorities against him and generated the resolve to destroy him. There is a perfect parallel here with the life stories of such people as Mohandas Gandhi and Martin Luther King.

Jesus challenged the established order. He did not cultivate the society of the rich and powerful, though he would probably have been welcome among them had he embraced their values. He did not abide by the accepted social and religious norms of his day. He set aside sabbath observance when he saw someone in need (Mk 3:1), and fasting laws when he saw greater good in eating and drinking with people. At meals he was not always careful to observe the proprieties of ritual purification (Mk 7). He challenged the reigning religious authorities directly for legalistically laying burdens on people and not lifting a finger to help, for consuming the substance of widows, for fasting and giving alms in public places just to be seen, for preferring strict observance in tiny matters of law to the larger demands of justice, mercy, and faith (Mt 23). He accused them also of killing the prophets God had sent them time and again to call them to conversion. In a symbolic gesture, he embarrassed them by making public protest against the commerce going on in the temple (Mk 12). He offended them further with his outrageous demand that the rich give up their holdings to relieve the sufferings of the poor. Like that of the prophets before him, Jesus' theology was political.

He attracted a great following. Just as he was offensive to those in power, he was very popular with those who were not. In him they saw the possibility of their liberation, and wanted to make him king (Jn 6:15). Jesus never accepted these offers, but he had come to pose such a social threat to the status quo that both Jewish and Roman authorities were well aware of him and very uneasy about him. In combination, they resolved to do away with him on criminal charges. The allegations were stirring up the people, opposing the tribute to Caesar, and making himself a king (Lk 23:2). The Roman governor Pilate could not find substantive cause, but gave way to pressure and had Jesus publicly flogged and executed (Lk 23:13). And so Jesus met his fate, crucified between two thieves.

It is chiefly liberation theology, originating in Latin America in the last several decades, which has opened our eyes to the intrinsic connection between Jesus' life and his death: that his death has this-worldly causes, that it is, in fact, almost predictable as the consequence of what he was doing. Prior to this insight, Jesus' life, teaching, and example were usually seen as having their own value and taught accordingly, while his death was viewed as having quite a distinct purpose, designed not on earth but in heaven: to make satisfaction to God for our sins.

What significance did Jesus himself see in his death, and what was his inner attitude toward it? Given the nature of gospel writing, that is very difficult to say. What we find much more of in the gospels and in Paul is the significance Jesus' followers saw in these events as they reflected on them. They saw the unjust death of a just man (Mk 15:39). They saw the tragic end of another prophet. They were reminded of the "servant" of the four servant songs in the prophetic writings of second Isaiah, songs about a godly man who ends up paying the price of other people's sinfulness and somehow brings healing to all by his sufferings (Is 42, 49, 50, 53). They saw his death, given the extraordinary quality of the life that preceded it, as a kind of perfect sacrifice offered to God which would make up for the sinfulness of the rest of us (1 Jn 2:2). They saw his death as causing a transformation in those touched by it and bringing about a broad diffusion of his spirit. In all they saw in it, they were heavily influenced, of course, by Jesus' resurrection, because that put the whole event in an entirely new light.

Regarding Jesus' own thoughts, we can only speculate. In the gospels we find him facing his death with some combination of anguish and trust. In the garden we see him struggling with fear and dread, yet emerging with a free subordination of his will to God's (Mk 14:32). On the cross, we hear the agonized cry of a person feeling abandoned by God (Mt 27:46), but his final word is one of trusting surrender (Lk 23:46). It is likely that Jesus saw this death coming. He probably predicted it, though perhaps not in the detail in which the gospels' three passion predictions have it. He must have realized that the only way he could avoid it was to drop out of public life or radically change what he was saying and doing. In conscience he felt he could do neither. That made it just a matter of time. Perhaps he saw in his death an opportunity to give final testimony to his trust in the faithful, loving God he had proclaimed. Perhaps he saw it as an opportunity to support us all by bearing his own suffering with dignity and hope. In both these respects, his death could be an act of love, a gift of himself to God and to his fellow human beings. Considerations such as these might be the basis of those sayings of his indicating that he positively wanted to lay down his life (Lk 13:33; Jn 14:31). He moves through his sham trial largely silent, and endures torture and the agony of death by crucifixion with just a few utterances.

For all of this, his death was felt as a great tragedy by those who followed him. Many feared for their own lives, and scattered as he fell. Those who stayed huddled together in desolation and fear, feeling all their hopes were dashed.

JESUS' RESURRECTION

The Fact of the Resurrection

It is against this bleak horizon that the resurrection dawns. Jesus is seen alive. At first his disciples are incredulous, but their unbelief becomes belief as witness after witness comes in. The gospel accounts of Jesus' appearances describe several scenes in which Jesus comes unexpectedly on a situation of discouragement and turns it into a celebration—on the women leaving the empty tomb (Mt 28), on Mary weeping at the tomb (Jn 20), on the disciples huddled in the upper room (Lk 24), on the two walking dejectedly back to Emmaus (Lk 24), on the disciples fishing without success (Jn 21). In his first letter to the Corinthians, Paul makes a list of people who saw the risen Jesus—Peter, the twelve, a group of five hundred, James, all the apostles, and finally himself, Paul, a man looking the other way (1 Cor 15:3-8).

Since none of us has ever experienced the resurrection of anyone from the dead, we might be disinclined to put any faith in these testimonies of an ancient people. This skepticism, reasonable as it is, has to contend with one rather massive fact. In the face of persecution and against great odds, Christianity rapidly became the dominant religion of the Roman empire. It is hard to imagine people going to their deaths by burning, crucifixion, wild beasts, or beheading, stoutly holding out for a resurrection they just imagined or dearly wished to be true. It is hard to imagine their taking this individual and his teachings seriously enough to build a literature and a movement around him when the religious authorities of the day condemned him as a blasphemer and troublemaker and put him to death. If Jesus had never been heard from after his crucifixion, we might have some written recollections of an interesting historical personage, but it seems most unlikely that we would have the church.

The Significance of the Resurrection

The resurrection of Jesus operates on several levels of significance. Reviewing them should make it clear why it is the cardinal affirmation of Christian faith.

1) *The resurrection validates all that Jesus said and did.* Jesus was a religious revolutionary. His claims about how God wanted to be served shocked the religious leaders of his day and divided the general populace. He revised the way his contemporaries thought about their scriptures. He laid claim to a very significant role in God's plan for human history. He insisted that God is loving, faithful, and merciful. He underscored God's concern for all who are oppressed by others, and God's desire that there be justice and life for all. All of this was called into question when he was crucified by the religious and political leaders of his society as a dangerous figure. Had there been no resurrection, we would be left wondering if Jesus was not deceived in his fundamental convictions. But God raised him from the dead. This was a decisive vindication.

2) *Only in the resurrection does Jesus attain the fullness of his personhood.* The life of Jesus was genuinely a development, as our lives are a development, and he reached his fullness only when he passed from this world to God. Only in the resurrection did Jesus realize the profundity of his union with God and the full significance of his life. In his appearing risen to his disciples, Jesus amazes them. He comes to them from glory, transformed, his divinity manifest. They have difficulty recognizing him, difficulty believing this is really he. They had known he was great, but did not think he was

that great. They had known he was close to God, but did not think he was *that* close to God. In the light of this experience of his splendor and transparency to God, they catch his full significance and can now recognize all those subtler hints of divinity present in his earthly life but not then fully grasped. So when they write the gospels, they embellish the earthly recollections with the truth they now experience. It is the Lord in the fullness of his stature that they portray as they recount the events of his historical life, because it is to that person that Christians now relate.

In a little noted passage, the Christian scriptures present the briefest summary of the career of Jesus seen as a process.

> Jesus *in the days of his flesh* offered prayers and supplications with loud cries and tears to the one who could save him from death, and he was heard because of *his reverence.* Although he was a son, he *learned obedience* through the things that he suffered; and *when he had been made perfect* he *became* the source of eternal salvation for all those who obey him, *designated by God* as high priest according to the order of Melchizedek (Heb 5:7-10, italics ours).

From this passage it seems that the earthly Jesus had to struggle with God, as we all do, had to learn obedience the hard way, as we all do, had to pass through trials and even the agony of death, trusting in spite of it all, as we all do, before he could become the source of unending salvation for others. In his resurrection he comes into the possession of that personhood which was being gradually fashioned all through his life by God's gifts and his own faithful responses.

3) *The resurrection is Jesus' transition into a new mode of existence: in the Christian community through the Spirit.*

There is another motif that runs through the Christian scriptures as they deal with the time after Jesus' death and resurrection. Jesus continues to live in the community of believers. He is with them always, among them and in each of them, present to them also in word and sacrament. This means he has attained a new mode of existing. The resurrection marks a transition from individual historical existence to a new spiritual presence in a whole community of persons.

This transition is the basis of Paul's theology of the church as body of Christ. When he speaks of it, notice how he practically identifies Christ and Spirit, indicating Jesus' new mode of being.

> The body is one and has many members, but all the members, many though they are, are one body; and so it is with Christ. It was in one Spirit that all of us, whether Jew or Greek, slave or free, were baptized into one body. All of us have been given to drink of the one Spirit....You (plural), then, are the body of Christ (1 Cor 12:12-27).

4) *The death/resurrection of Jesus is a paradigm which illumines the riddle of existence.* What is most baffling about human life is all the suffering we undergo—the toil, the frustrations, the injustices, the losses, the struggles. So heavy is all this at times that life seems meaningless, joyless, hopeless.

The death/resurrection of Jesus is not just something that happens to *him.* It is larger than that. It is a paradigm, i.e., a model which serves as a principle of interpretation. It helps us understand the puzzle of our own suffering and death and gives us a basis for hope as we pass through them. In doing that, it saves us. It reveals that our suffering and dying are not final, but are a passage to some kind of new life, as Jesus' suffering and dying were for him. In this climactic moment of his career, Jesus demonstrates in action what he had previously proclaimed as the central paradox of the gospel:

> Unless the grain of wheat falls into the ground and dies,
> it remains just a grain; but if it dies, it bears much fruit
> (Jn 12:24).

And in another place:

> Those who want to save their lives will lose them; but
> those who lose their lives for the sake of me and the
> gospel will save them (Mk 8:35).

There are many seed parables in the gospels (e.g., Mk 13). All
of them depict a planting which results in the death of seeds
as they were, and the outbreak of something greater and
more abundant. So it is in the death/resurrection of Jesus,
which thus becomes the basis of Christian insight and hope.
What it reveals is that God works within the mystery of our
suffering to bring good out of evil, meaning out of absurdity,
life out of death.

With these considerations we can perhaps now see two
Christian truths. The death and resurrection of Jesus are not
two isolated events in mere succession, but rather one complex event—a passage with a dark side and a bright side to it,
both filled with significance. And the death/resurrection of
Jesus is the cardinal affirmation of Christian faith, the central
Christian mystery, the climax and epitome of all that Jesus
was about.

SUMMARY

The brief life of Jesus of Nazareth has had enormous
impact on the world. Brilliant in his teaching and beautiful in
the way he moved among people, Jesus has become pivotal in
the way a large segment of humanity relates to God and to life.
He is seen as the fullest expression of divinity and the model
of humanity. The outstanding traits in his life were his union
with God and his service of others. He summed up his teach-

ing in one great commandment which reflects this orienta-
tion: that we love God with our whole heart and our neighbor
as ourself. Because he confronted the reigning authorities of
his time on several scores, and because his life and teaching
were so revolutionary in their implications, Jesus was executed. But God vindicated him, raising him from death and causing him to be seen by many. This extraordinary event was the
beginning of the Christian community called church, in
whose members the risen Jesus continues to dwell as Lord.

Questions and Exercises

1. Who is Jesus in the lives of Christians?

2. What are the outstanding features of the life and teaching of
    Jesus?

3. Why was Jesus killed?

4. What is the lasting significance of the death and resurrection
    of Jesus for Christians?

5. How closely does the portrait of Jesus presented in this
    chapter correspond with the portrait you have?

6. What importance, if any, does Jesus have for your life?

7. Ask various Christians you know what role Jesus plays in their
    lives. What do you learn?

Suggestions for Further Reading

Marcus Borg, *Jesus: A New Vision* (Harper, 1987). A fresh
perspective on Jesus' significance for our times.

Raymond Brown, *An Introduction to New Testament Christology*
(Paulist, 1994). Makes New Testament scholarship available to a
broad audience, showing how Jesus was understood in New
Testament times.

Elizabeth Johnson, *Consider Jesus: Waves of Renewal in Christology* (Crossroad, 1990). Summarizes recent thinking on Jesus.

Albert Nolan, *Jesus before Christianity* (Orbis, 1992). A fresh interpretation of Jesus from a liberation perspective by a priest theologian in South Africa.

John O'Grady, *Models of Jesus Revisited.* Revised edition (Paulist, 1994). Offers and evaluates six different models used by Christians today in relating to Jesus.

William Reiser, *Talking about Jesus Today: An Introduction to the Story behind Our Faith* (Paulist, 1993). A college theology teacher shows how to enter the gospel story imaginatively and prayerfully to learn about Jesus by following him.

Jon Sobrino, *Jesus the Liberator: A Historical-Theological View* (Orbis, 1993). A prominent liberation theologian from El Salvador presents a contemporary Christology rooted in the experience of the oppressed.

Maryanne Stevens, *Reconstructing the Christ Symbol: Essays in Feminist Christology* (Paulist, 1993). Six feminist theologians proclaim Jesus as the reversal of status systems and source of human liberation for all.

R.S. Sugirtharajah, ed., *Asian Faces of Jesus* (Orbis, 1993). Asian scholars employ new interpretive resources, cultural symbols, and thought patterns to make sense of Jesus for their time and place.

CHAPTER 6

Faith

Faith is so central to Christian life that the Acts of the Apostles commonly uses the term "believers" to designate members of the Christian community. To become a Christian is to believe. Jesus makes clear that faith is essential to hearing his message and receiving his gifts.

However, the fact that faith is central does not mean that it is easy to understand or embrace. The gospels are filled with people who puzzle over the demands of faith. Just as they have questions about faith, so do we. What exactly does it mean to believe? What enables one person to say "I believe in Jesus Christ" while others hear his message and walk away? What can a thoughtful person be expected to believe in our age? We are disturbed when we find ourselves questioning one or another aspect of our faith. Sometimes too, unable to answer questions put to us by others, we fear our faith is too naive for the complexities of modern life.

Every generation of Christians formulates faith in Jesus in the midst of changing historical circumstances. One development particularly important for faith today is the religious pluralism which offers each individual a variety of spiritual doctrines and trends. Both individuals and groups can more easily retain confidence in a belief system when they are shielded from other views. When exposed to competing beliefs it is more difficult to determine what in fact we do believe.

Since life as a Christian requires an understanding of the meaning of faith, this chapter explores four questions frequently asked about it: 1) What does it mean to believe? 2) Why do even believers experience unbelief and doubt? 3) Is there any assurance that our beliefs are true? and 4) Does faith change during a person's lifetime?

WHAT DOES IT MEAN TO BELIEVE?

Faith as Ultimate Concern

In the 1950s, Protestant theologian Paul Tillich published *The Dynamics of Faith*, a small book that has become a classic. In it he uses a broad definition to describe faith: the state of being ultimately concerned. We are, of course, concerned about many things: our school work or job, family, friends. Among these preoccupations are also spiritual concerns, some of which become the center of our existence. Faith is not always religious in its content. Things like success, social standing, or economic power can become gods in our lives, making total and urgent claims. Whatever absorbs the energies of our hearts and minds is, in fact, our ultimate concern. Tillich believes we often make passing values the center of our lives. The book of Deuteronomy, echoed by Jesus, tells us what should be ultimate: "You shall love the Lord your God with all your heart, and with all your soul, and with all your might" (6:5).

Faith as ultimate concern involves both content and personal commitment: there is something that concerns us ultimately (content) and our concern is itself ultimate (commitment). To get in touch with the centers of value and power that sustain our lives, we might ask:

What causes, goals, or institutions receive my best time
and energy?

What power or powers do I fear and trust?

To what or whom am I committed?

In other words, discovering the object of our faith means
asking ourselves on what we center our heart, what values are
the focus of our lives, what things concern us most deeply.
Since no one is truly without ultimate concern, Tillich's
definition makes faith a quality of every human life. It is not
then a question of those who do not have faith and those who
do. The issue is: Is our commitment to something finite or to
something transcendent and ultimate?

When the bible refers to the commitment of faith, it
speaks of trust or unshakable confidence. Biblical faith
means committing ourselves to someone wholly and without
reserve. We are willing to risk our whole being for that
person. Abraham is held up as a model of faith in the Hebrew
scriptures because he trusts in God even when he cannot
clearly see what this means or where such faith will take him
(Gen 12; Rom 4). Sarah trusts that the God who promised her
a son will be faithful to that promise in spite of her age, and
she becomes the mother of many descendants (Heb 11:11-
12). Confidence in God enables Moses and his sister Miriam
to lead their people out of slavery in Egypt (Ex 15). The
gospels likewise portray faith as person to person trust. A
woman with a hemorrhage is certain that if she but touches
the hem of Jesus' garment she will be cured (Lk 8:43-48). A
man who is asking Jesus to cure his epileptic son cries out, "I
believe, Lord; help my unbelief" (Mk 9:14-29). The Hebrew
trust in God has thus become focused in Jesus. Scripture
makes clear the power of such faith. Jesus says it is the
condition which makes healing possible: "Your faith has
made you whole" (Mk 5:34).

Faith is a free decision on our part, but it is also a gift of God. This too is a very important dimension of it. God takes the initiative with us, and faith is our response. In all the instances just cited, God has acted upon the persons involved and they are responding with their trust, commitment, obedience. God has manifested self and offered self for a relationship. Paul frequently emphasizes in his writings how faith is a gift of God, something to be thankful for. His own conversion is a fine example of it. He was so powerfully seized by God he could hardly say no. Most of us are not that dramatically accosted, but religious experience is always part of the basis of our faith. Whether it be in nature, our personal history, a passage of scripture, or a charismatic person, God speaks first, and then we are faced with a choice. Because faith is a gift as well as a choice, it makes sense to pray for it if we feel we want it but cannot get all the way there, or when we feel our faith is weak.

Faith as a Commitment of the Total Person

Describing faith as ultimate concern is one way of answering the question, What does it mean to believe? Another way to approach the question is to consider how our person is involved in an act of faith. We may have learned to see faith as an act simply of the intellect, an assent to truths which we cannot fully understand. Perhaps we think of faith primarily in terms of the will, as something we make ourselves do even though it may be difficult. But faith is not an action simply of the intellect, the will, or the emotions. It is, rather, a movement of the total person.

A comparison with human relationships helps us understand this. God's revelation is an offer of friendship, and faith is a personal response to this gift. Like any friendship, it engages the whole person in some way. When we respond in human friendship, we think and choose and feel; our whole person is engaged. The same is true of a relationship with Jesus. While Christian faith implies acceptance of certain truths, such acceptance is not identical with faith itself.

In order to make clear that Christian faith is more than the acceptance of certain dogmas, a distinction is sometimes made between *faith and belief*. Faith is a relationship with God which engages our total personhood. It is a commitment of the whole person in love and loyalty to what is perceived as transcendent value. Beliefs are the doctrines, facts, or content of faith, in other words, the intellectual dimension of faith. They are imperfect attempts to express aspects of faith, to translate faith into concepts that aid fuller understanding. We can therefore refer to belief as the holding of certain ideas.

It is at the intellectual level that theology operates. Theology is not the same as faith. It is reflection on faith. In struggling with this problem centuries ago, St. Anselm spoke of theology as "faith seeking understanding." Theology helps us to understand and justify our faith. It enables us to make a well-founded and responsible decision. For example, I may be drawn to belief in Jesus as a figure of central importance for my life. As I reflect on the act of total personal trust I have placed in him, I may turn to theology for answers to certain questions that arise: What is the meaning of the salvation Jesus offers? How can we relate the human and the divine in his life? How are we to understand the miracles of Jesus? Theologians attempt to answer such questions anew in each era, and so clarify the meaning of Christian beliefs.

We described faith as a total commitment to what we value most in life. When Christ is the center of our existence we speak of Christian faith. Christian faith is the response of our whole being to the revelation of God in Jesus Christ.

WHY DO EVEN BELIEVERS EXPERIENCE UNBELIEF AND DOUBT?

In considering how unbelief differs from belief, we must first acknowledge that elements of both exist in each of us. Many people identify unbelief with professed atheism. However, unbelief exists within as well as outside of the Christian community. In fact, it often masquerades as apparent belief. Since faith involves a commitment of one's whole person, it is not enough simply to state that one is a believer. The gospel writers do not portray Jesus as excessively concerned with Greco-Roman paganism. Rather, it is the unbelief of his disciples that concerns him. As the historian of religion Martin Marty notes, unbelief really describes our sustained attempts to create fullness of life apart from God. A church or nation may give lip service to faith in Jesus, while actually resting its hope and action on consumer goods or nuclear weapons.

Cultural religion is another name for this kind of unbelief. For long periods of Christian history we had a phenomenon known as cultural Christianity. People belonged to the Christian community by virtue of their birth into a family or nation. Much of France was Catholic. Many sections of Germany were Lutheran. But many who called themselves Christian under these circumstances had little understanding of Christian faith or personal commitment to the gospel. In the 19th century Søren Kierkegaard attacked what he called "Christendom." He believed that in his native Denmark there were millions of nominal Christians who had never been touched by the real force of the gospel. Karl Rahner reminds us that this era of cultural Christianity has come to a close. Rahner believes that in the future we will see a reduction in the number of Christians, since only those who choose to belong in a committed way will now be numbered as Christians. Adult faith is a personal decision, beyond culture or family.

Some people equate doubt about their faith with unbelief. But doubts are a natural part of any faith that is alive and growing. When people experience doubts, they sometimes fear that they are losing their faith. The French novelist, Georges Bernanos, commented that we do not lose our faith; it simply ceases to influence our lives. Since faith is a personal relationship, it loses its vigor when it is no longer nurtured. When daily events crowd out all reference to God, all worship, all prayer, faith drifts to the backroads of the mind.

What feels like the loss of faith may in fact be a movement out of the limits of one form of faith. Faith is not an act that occurs just once and is finished. Rather it is a living relationship which must continue to grow. The occasion for such growth may be an experience of disillusionment with previous forms of faith. This disillusionment leads to more adequate understandings, even if the new understandings seem less clear and simple than the old. It may be a crisis experience, such as a personal accident or loss, that alters the way one believes. Many students who leave home for the first time to attend college find that much of what they had believed was, in fact, their parents' convictions, not their own. Perhaps they attended church services with their family and now, left to their own choice, find they no longer go to church. They see their faith challenged by a new environment with new questions and decisions. In an effort to build a faith-life of their own, they may reject much of what they had been taught.

As Karl Rahner emphasizes, faith is always at risk. A faith that is growing along with the other dimensions of our lives will continually face doubts as new questions arise. Doubt, then, can be evidence that we are willing to grow. It is the price we pay for new insights, for remaining intellectually and spiritually alive. Only with the death of previous levels of faith can new and more adequate ones arise.

This mixture of belief and unbelief within the life of a believing Christian is powerfully illustrated by the life of Dag Hammarskjöld, former secretary general of the United Nations. Hammarskjöld died in a plane crash while he was on a UN mission in the Congo and Katanga in 1961. After his death a diplomat friend and a lawyer flew to his Manhattan apartment to dispose of his personal belongings. Beside his bed they found a stack of about 200 typed pages held in a clipboard, marked "personal." The pages turned out to be a diary of about 600 entries with a title page added: markings, blazes, trail marks. This diary, later published as *Markings*, recounts Hammarskjöld's groping journey into faith. Hammarskjöld was a man with a skeptical mind. He struggled not only with self-doubt but with doubts about God. *Markings* reveals his journey to the center of his self where he discovered God. In spite of his doubts he was able to say yes to life and to God. He came to see Jesus as one who had set out to live the role assigned to him without benefit of superhuman knowledge or aid. Accepting life as a risky venture, Hammarskjöld came gradually to a readiness to walk the same road of possibility which Jesus walked.

We have explored several possible answers to our question, Why do even believers experience unbelief and doubt? There is inauthentic faith, a claim to believe when one's life does not support that claim. On the other hand, as is clear from the life of Dag Hammarskjöld, doubts and questions are an integral part of the Christian's faith journey.

IS THERE ANY ASSURANCE THAT OUR BELIEFS ARE TRUE?

Kinds of Truth

Christians are often troubled by truth questions. Did the miracles of Jesus really happen? Are the gospels reliable? How can I base my life on an event like the resurrection which can only be verified with greater or lesser certitude? When the reasons for our belief begin to seem less convincing than they once did, we fear that our faith may have no real foundation.

There is more than one kind of truth involved in questions of faith. When we ask whether something actually happened, we are inquiring after historical truth. We sometimes equate the truth of faith with this kind of truth. If something really happened, then we can believe it. Did Adam and Eve really exist? Did Jonah really live three days in the belly of the whale? For some the ideal is not so much historical truth as it is scientific certainty. We can trust only what we can observe and measure.

Important as historical and scientific truth are, they are not the only kinds of truth. There is also the truth of poetry, story, and drama. When Shakespeare writes *Hamlet*, it is surely to communicate truth—though Hamlet never lived. The play conveys not just one but many truths, deep insights into human life, though the play is not historical. When Adrienne Rich writes a love poem, she brilliantly conveys the truth of the experience of being in love. Her poem is neither history nor science. It is a different kind of truth she wishes to express, and she chooses poetry as most apt for expressing it. The better songs we hear on the radio stir our feelings and deepen our insight into life. They too convey truth.

When we turn to the bible with awareness of the different kinds of truth, we recognize that the book of Genesis is not concerned with scientific statements; rather, through poetry and story it teaches profound religious truths about the goodness of creation and God as the source of all being. Jesus' parables such as the good Samaritan (Lk 10:25-37) and the prodigal son (Lk 15:11-32) are stories he created to convey the heart of the gospel message concerning God's love and the Christian call to compassion and forgiveness.

These are not lesser kinds of truth; they are a different, and sometimes deeper, kind. When we are asking about the truth of our beliefs, then, it is important to begin by recognizing these many kinds of truth. Religious truth need not necessarily meet our modern criteria of historical and scientific accuracy to be a solid basis for faith.

Truth in Action

In reflecting on the relationship between truth and faith, it is also helpful to realize that faith is a lived truth. It is a way of *being or relating* to God and others. Arguments play a role in faith, but they are not the heart of it. Lived experience is. As we saw in Chapter 2, John Henry Newman addressed this question. His writings reflect both respect for intellectual inquiry and recognition of the limits of reason. He saw that you could not make someone believe simply by presenting arguments for the faith. While these arguments may be important to the process of one's developing faith, faith is not the conclusion of an argument. According to Newman, it is action that gives faith its verification. When we are personally involved in some question, slight evidence can move us to action. When we are not so involved, even a great deal of evidence leaves us unmoved. Newman illustrates this point with an example: Even if we knew that the planet Jupiter were in flames, we might go on with life as usual. But even a dubious cry of fire at night will rouse us from our beds. Newman urges his listeners to live in such a way as to discover the truth of faith. In other words, to our question, Is there any assurance that our beliefs are true? Newman responds that such assurance does not come from detached questioning but rather from trying out the truth in action.

We see this characteristic of faith in people who encounter Jesus in the gospels. Meeting Jesus is an experience which transforms them. But they cannot give a complete explanation of it. It is not just a matter of the powerful signs Jesus works. Rather, they are living their way into faith as they follow him, with openness to the presence and power of God at work in him.

This emphasis on the intrinsic link between faith and action is also found in the contemporary movement called liberation theology. Liberation theologians such as Gustavo Gutiérrez and María Pilar Aquino are not concerned so much with developing theological systems as with creating new ways of living and acting in the world. They distinguish between "orthodoxy," or correct belief, and "orthopraxis," correct action. "Praxis" here refers to a kind of reflection and action aimed at transforming the world. In the past the emphasis has been more exclusively on orthodoxy, correct belief. What is needed now is stress on the balancing perspective that truth is in action. A central concern of liberation theology is how Christian love can be made effective in history.

Gutiérrez has said that to know God is to do justice: whoever tries seriously to live justly with others is on the way to God. Love of God is necessarily expressed through love of neighbor, and our neighbor is not only individual persons, but also whole peoples, especially those suffering misery and oppression. María Pilar Aquino seeks to create new ways of living together in society that enable women as well as men to achieve human integrity. Jon Sobrino, a Spanish Jesuit who has worked for many years in Central America, finds this link between truth and action in the biblical description of faith: to know the truth is to do the truth; to know Jesus is to follow Jesus. In other words, liberation theology emphasizes that it is the real following of Jesus, especially in his concern for the poor, which brings knowledge of the truth of Jesus and his message.

We have attempted to answer our initial question about the truth of our faith by expanding the meaning of truth. There are many kinds of truth, and the truth of Christian faith is learned most fully in action. We discover that our faith is true as we live it out and find that it works, i.e., it bears good fruit, it gives our lives energy and purpose, it is confirmed by many different things that happen as we live it.

DOES FAITH CHANGE DURING A PERSON'S LIFETIME?

Faith Development Theory

We have always been aware of certain physical and psychological developments that take place as we move from childhood through adolescence to adulthood and old age. During our century these stages of the human life cycle have been more carefully studied and described in the writing of psychologists such as Jean Piaget and Erik Erikson. Erikson shows that the human personality unfolds gradually over the course of one's entire life-span. There is a pattern to this unfolding, certain predictable challenges and responses that occur at each stage, even though the process differs somewhat from person to person. For example, in adolescence the question "Who am I?" is central. One's identity is the focus of special concern. During early and middle adulthood other questions become paramount: Whom am I with, and how am I with them? Issues of intimacy arise at this time in experiences of friendship and love.

Since faith involves our total personality, faith also changes during the course of our lives. Reflection shows us that the faith of our college years differs from that of our high school days and from how we believed as a child. Recently more attention has been paid to just how faith grows through the life cycle. James Fowler, a psychologist of religion, building on the theories of Piaget and Erikson, has elaborated a series of developmental faith stages in his *Stages of Faith* and *Becoming Adult, Becoming Christian*. Faith stages represent significant changes in the way we know and value, and therefore in the way we formulate and respond to life's unfolding meaning.

Fowler, like Tillich, describes faith as a universal human experience. In other words, we live by faith, by forming and being formed in images and attitudes toward life's ultimate conditions. Fowler's study focuses on how we compose these guiding images of existence and shape our lives in relation to ultimate values. Images of ultimacy center in causes, persons, or goals that promise to give our lives meaning, security or nobility. For Christians, this center of existence is the life and message of Jesus.

Fowler's stages relate to the structure of our faith rather than its contents, to *how* we believe more than *what* we believe. He names many experiences we vaguely recognize but cannot clearly describe. As we will see, most of his stages concern the development of our image of God.

Fowler's Stages of Faith

Primal Faith: There is a pre-stage which Fowler calls primal or undifferentiated faith. This stage describes an infant's relationship with the environment as the infant gradually recognizes that the environment is distinct from the self. Children's first pre-images of God are formed from their interaction with primary caregivers. In a vague and often unconscious way, the quality and consistency of their care leads to trust or distrust of the world and themselves.

1) *Intuitive-Projective Faith:* This first stage typically forms between the ages of two and six or seven, as children acquire language and their imaginations come to life. They

notice the gestures, rituals, and words adults use in their language of faith, and form their own notions of God from them. Children see the ultimate in concrete symbols and images found in bible stories, fairy tales, or pictures, and combine fragments of these stories and images into their own associations dealing with God and the sacred. A six-year-old boy in one of Fowler's interviews, when asked where heaven is, says that it is high, high, high, up in the sky, and God is there with the wise men who are dead. A four-and-a-half-year-old girl, whose parents have intentionally avoided exposing her to religious symbols, says she believes in God because people in shows like "Leave It To Beaver" believe in God. Other sources of her knowledge of God include wedding and funeral scenes found occasionally in TV westerns.

2) *Mythic-Literal Faith:* This stage usually takes form between the ages of seven and twelve, about the time a child starts school. The most important development at this stage is the ability to bind our experiences into meaning through narratives. We have a better sense of space, time, and causality and so are able to tell our own stories and retell the stories we are told. We want to know the faith stories of our family or community. Symbols and beliefs are appropriated with literal interpretations, for example, the belief that God is Father, Son and Holy Spirit may be interpreted to mean that God is in three parts. We see reciprocal fairness as the principle which governs divine-human relations: good actions are rewarded and evil is punished. A fourth-grade girl describes God as an old man with a white beard and white hair wearing a long robe, who sees people trying, and is merciful. He does what he thinks is right and tries to do the best.

3) *Synthetic-Conventional Faith:* Around twelve, another change occurs for most young people. This third stage is called synthetic because we are trying to pull together

different elements into a unity or synthesis. A new self-consciousness develops and with it an awareness of the images of ourselves which we believe significant others in our lives hold of us. We struggle to draw together or integrate all these available reflections and mirrorings of our self into a unified identity. We also try to pull together into a unity the stories, values, and beliefs that we discover in our relationships. This means that faith is conventional, formed in reliance upon others, either peers or adults. The expectations and judgments of significant others are very important at this stage, as there is not enough grasp of one's identity to maintain an independent perspective. God is reimaged as knowing those mysterious depths of self and others which we cannot know. There is a hunger for a God who knows, accepts, and confirms the self deeply, a divine significant other. A fifteen-year-old girl in her interview describes God as always there. When she struggles with a problem she feels that God cares. God is a personal companion and guide who knows and loves her. The authority for her religious and moral beliefs still lies principally with her parents.

Many adults continue in this stage of faith well beyond adolescence or young adulthood. In fact, Fowler believes most adults are at this stage of development. The transition to the next stage requires a new quality of personal responsibility for our values and for membership in community. Many factors lead people to resist invitations to this degree of responsibility.

4) *Individuative-Reflective Faith:* At about twenty, some young persons move from the synthetic-conventional stage to one in which their self-reflection is no longer so dependent on others' perceptions of them. They are able to take a critical look at the commitments, lifestyle, beliefs, and attitudes they have previously taken for granted, and to fashion a more personal and reflective faith. Since it requires

a shift from reliance on external sources of authority, this examination of self and values is frequently precipitated by the experience of "leaving home"—emotionally or physically, or both—through travel, entering college, or joining the service. The judgments, expectations, advice and counsel of others remain important, but persons at this stage reserve the right to choose and to take responsibility for their choices. Membership in communities is now chosen rather than being merely a matter of inheritance. The transition to this stage represents an upheaval in one's life, and its process can last five to seven years or longer.

5) *Conjunctive Faith:* Some adults find that after age thirty-five, in mid-life, they reach a stage where they are able to integrate the apparent contradictions in their experience of themselves, society, and ultimate reality. There is a new awareness of the need to face and hold together the polar tensions of life: being both young and old, both masculine and feminine, both constructive and destructive. Fowler says he finds it hard to describe this stage clearly, but he gives some analogies which might help. The transition from Stage 4 to Stage 5 is something like looking at a field of flowers simultaneously through a microscope and a wide-angle lens. It is also like discovering that one's parents are remarkable people not just because they are one's parents. With this perspective we are able to appreciate our own as well as others' viewpoints. In other words, Stage 5 moves beyond either/or thinking; it is a way of seeing many sides of an issue simultaneously. Stage 5 recognizes that truth has more dimensions than most accounts recognize. Persons at this stage, while strongly committed to their traditions, recognize that the symbols, stories, doctrines, and liturgies of those traditions are necessarily partial. They are therefore interested now in learning from other traditions which they previously saw as threatening.

6) *Universalizing Faith:* This is a stage few attain. Persons Fowler considers representative of it are Gandhi, Martin Luther King, Jr. in the last years of his life, and Mother Teresa of Calcutta. They see themselves as part of the universe of all being to which their loyalties are committed. We experience these people as revolutionary in their perspectives and care because of their love of all being and their genuine self-transcendence. By teaching or quiet example, they call us to righteousness and to wider, less self- or group-centered faith. They have an enlarged vision of justice and a more comprehensive awareness of truth.

We opened this section with the question, Does faith change during a person's lifetime? Faith development theory tries to show us that faith is a living, growing thing. The call of Christian faith is to an ever deepening synthesis of all our experience and to ever widening circles of love.

SUMMARY

Faith is the state of being ultimately concerned, and hence is a universal human experience. One's ultimate concern or center of value can be many different things. Christian faith is centered on Jesus' life and message. Faith is a total personal commitment, and so it involves not only the intellect but all aspects of the person. The formulation of beliefs and the reflections of theologians meet our need to understand and explain our lived commitment.

Unbelief takes many forms, and can exist within as well as outside of the Christian community. Because faith involves risk and growth, we will probably experience doubts as we move from one level of faith to another or face personal life crises. Confidence in the truth of our Christian faith means recognizing the many kinds of truth, including the truth of poetry and story, and seeking verification through action.

Faith development theory helps us understand the challenges and evolution we experience as our faith changes over the course of a life-span.

Questions and Exercises

1. Explain Tillich's definition of faith as ultimate concern, and name some of those realities most likely to become ultimate concerns for people today.

2. Do you agree or disagree with Tillich's description of faith? Why?

3. What is your own ultimate concern?

4. Why is it important to realize that faith is a commitment of the total person? Explain the relationship between faith and belief, and faith and theology.

5. Do you agree that unbelief can mask itself as belief? How can this happen with nations as well as individuals?

6. Show how the experience of doubt can lead to a deepening of faith. Have you had personal experience of this?

7. Name and briefly explain the different kinds of truth mentioned in this chapter. What kind of truth do you consider most important to the certitude of faith?

8. Do you find yourself identifying with any of Fowler's stages of faith? Which ones?

9. Look back over your own life of faith and note any changes you are aware of, for example, in your images of God or your reliance on external authority to support your faith. Recall any stories that were important to your faith at different points in your life.

Suggestions for Further Reading

Martin Copenhaver, *Living Faith While Holding Doubts* (Pilgrim Press, 1989). A Protestant pastor grapples with the problem of faith and doubt.

Allan Figueroa Deck, ed., *Frontiers of Hispanic Theology in the United States* (Orbis, 1992). Essays by women and men on faith as rooted in the cultures, histories, and hopes of Hispanic people in the U.S.

Avery Dulles, *The Assurance of Things Hoped For: A Theology of Faith* (Oxford University, 1994). A leading contemporary theologian gives an overview of the literature on faith, and presents his own understanding of it.

James W. Fowler, *Becoming Adult, Becoming Christian* (Harper and Row, 1984). Applies his research and theories on the development of faith to the Christian vocation.

Catherine Mowry LaCugna, ed., *Freeing Theology: The Essentials of Theology in Feminist Perspective* (HarperSanFrancisco, 1992). Ten women theologians show what it means to do theology from a new perspective, treating topics such as method, revelation, Christ, and church.

Paul Tillich, *Dynamics of Faith* (Harper and Row, 1957). An introduction to the meaning of faith and its relationship to doubt, community, symbol, truth, and courage.

Mary Jo Weaver, *Springs of Water in a Dry Land: Spiritual Survival for Catholic Women Today* (Beacon, 1992). Presents strategies to help women maintain faith and hope in the midst of oppression.

CHAPTER 7

The Mystery of Suffering and Evil

The contemporary fiction writer, Elie Wiesel, poses in powerful terms the modern question of God's relationship to human suffering and evil. Wiesel, a Hungarian Jew, was deported with his family to Auschwitz when he was a boy, and then to Buchenwald, where his parents and a younger sister died. In *Night*, Wiesel's memoir of these experiences, he describes the death of God in his soul as he confronts the evil of these concentration camps. It is not God's existence that he doubts, but God's justice. His agony over God's apparent silence is movingly described in a central scene in *Night*. An innocent young child is being hanged by the S.S., and as he dies Wiesel hears a man behind him cry out, "Where is God? Where is He?"

This man's cry is echoed by many who agonize today over the problem of human suffering and evil. The senseless murder of innocent people, the sexual abuse of children, the scale of world hunger, the ravages of constant war, the devastation of earthquakes and other natural disasters, the pain of disease and the agony of death—all these realities wrench our hearts and minds, challenging our faith at its roots. Can it be that God could do something about this suffering and chooses not to? Then how can such a creator be described as a God of love? Or is it possible that God is unable to prevent such occurrences? Then what becomes of the God of power in whom we have always believed?

Throughout the centuries the existence of suffering and evil in the world has been a major stumbling block to faith. The Russian novelist Fyodor Dostoevsky raises the question in *The Brothers Karamazov*, the novel which is the culmination of his life and themes. Dostoevsky describes himself as a child of his age, an age in which faith is no longer easy for us. In the novel, Ivan Karamazov expresses these struggles of faith. In one scene Ivan visits his brother Alyosha in the monastery where Alyosha is a novice. Ivan tells Alyosha he is unable to accept God's world because of the terrible wickedness and suffering it contains. "I recognize in all humility," says Ivan, "that I cannot understand why the world is arranged as it is." He understands that human beings have been given freedom, but he questions whether it is worthwhile. Is freedom worth the tears of one suffering child? No, he says. Even universal forgiveness and happiness in the future will not make it worth such sufferings. So he gives back his entrance ticket. "It's not God that I don't accept, Alyosha, only I most respectfully return Him the ticket."

Any consideration of the foundations of Christian faith must respond to these questions about God's relationship to human suffering and evil. We will explore this issue in two parts: first, the more general attempts made to solve the problem; and second, the message and activity of Jesus in relation to evil and suffering.

ATTEMPTS TO EXPLAIN SUFFERING AND EVIL

The Books of Job and Genesis

The book of Job in the Hebrew scriptures conveys the traditional religious explanations for human suffering, and illustrates as well the inadequacy of these answers. As the story begins, Job has everything: health, wealth, family, friends. Gradually he loses them, and he ends up a broken man on a dung heap, taunted by his friends. Why has all this happened? His friends trot out the traditional explanations. Job must have sinned, for suffering is a divine punishment for sin: "Can you recall a guiltless person that perished, or have you ever seen good people brought to nothing" (Job 4:7)? Their other explanation is that Job's suffering is a testing, a disciplining of the human spirit: "Happy the person whom God corrects" (Job 5:17)! In other words, Job suffers because he deserves it, or because it is good for him in some way. But Job protests his innocence, and his friends' answers do nothing to lift the veil of mystery from his suffering. Despite their inadequacy, the answers presented by Job's friends continue to be offered to people who suffer.

As the book of Job reaches its climax, God speaks to Job from the midst of the whirlwind. God does not answer Job's questions or respond to the theories of his three friends. Job does not learn why the righteous suffer, why there is evil in God's world, or why justice is thwarted. God poses instead a series of unanswerable questions, revealing the inscrutable designs of the divine majesty and testifying to a reality other than that of absurdity and suffering:

> Where were you when I laid the earth's foundations?
> Tell me, since you are so well informed.
> Who decided the dimensions of it, do you know (38:4)?
>
> Have you ever in your life given orders to the morning
> or sent the dawn to its post (38:12)?
>
> Have you journeyed all the way to the sources of the sea,
> or walked where the abyss is deepest (38:16)?

With these and other questions, God unfolds before Job the beauty and paradox of creation, and sends home the point that Job is in waters way over his head. It is as if Job cried out, "God, I don't understand!" And God said, "That's right, Job, you don't understand!" And hearing this, Job is comforted. He begins to see that suffering does not negate God's goodness or the value of life. After this encounter with the awesome Mystery, Job says:

> I had known you only by hearsay;
> but now, having seen you with my own eyes,
> I retract all I have said,
> and in dust and ashes I repent (Job 42:5-6).

Job's questions are not answered—except by an overwhelming personal experience of God's transcendence and presence in all of nature.

Another biblical book reflects on the root of evil in the world. The book of Genesis, in its creation accounts, declares that the world as it came from the hand of God was good: "God saw all that was made, and indeed it was very good" (Gen 1:31). The evil in the world is not from God, but rather results from a misuse of human freedom. Later thinkers develop this insight. In choosing to create a world where freedom exists, God chose a limitation of divine power. Freedom to love includes the freedom to hate. Freedom to choose the good necessarily implies the freedom to choose evil. God then chooses to be limited in all the areas in which this freedom operates: human moral choice, the evolution of human nature, the freedom of a world in evolution on a cosmic level.

The book of Genesis describes creation as the replacing of chaos with order.

> In the beginning God created the heavens and the earth. Now the earth was a formless void, there was darkness over the deep, and God's spirit hovered over the water (Gen 1:1-2).

Some current explanations speak of this process of creating order from chaos as still going on. On the total level of creation, we have a world in process. It is an organic world of growth and change where freedom is also involved at every level. There is a certain amount of randomness and chance in such a world. Not all things happen with purpose. To accept this explanation of evil entails accepting that element of chance, relinquishing some of our conviction that all things are ordered. It means believing that a world of life, growth, and eventual happiness is worth the price exacted by this combination of order and chance.

The Power of Sin and Evil

We see evidence of the reality of created freedom every day in the destructive and constructive deeds of others, the actions of hate that tear apart the fabric of human existence, and those of love which heal it. Sin or moral evil is the use of this capacity for free decision in ways that destroy our relationship with self, others and God—in fact, with all of creation. This destruction of our capacity for relatedness and the subsequent need for reconciliation is the basic biblical description of sin. Whether it takes shape as envy, racism, or infidelity, sin is always in some way a denial of the love we should have toward ourselves, one another, and God.

In addition to personal sins, there is also a larger power of sin at work in the world which impedes and limits our freedom. Just as there is a power of holiness that precedes our personal decisions, qualifying and conditioning them, so there is a state of sinfulness that conditions our moral lives. For example, we encounter bad example, sometimes also with pressure to go along; some values, such as honesty and courage, may be obscured or totally absent from our environment. Theologians call this universal influence of sin the "sin of the world" or original sin.

Classical, Process, and Feminist Theologies

The explanations presented so far focus on the *source* of evil and suffering in the world, and attempt to answer the question, Where do they come from? Other explanations respond to a related question, Can God do anything about this suffering and evil? Attempts to answer this question explore the problem of God's power in relation to evil.

Tradition describes God as all-powerful. But it has proved difficult to attribute all power to God without also implicating that divine power in some way in the existence of evil. Classical approaches, such as those of Augustine and Thomas Aquinas, make two distinctions in an effort to solve the problem:

1) *They deny any real being to evil.* They insist that all that is, is good. Evil is non-being. It is not a substance and has no nature. Evil is the *lack* or deprivation of a perfection which should be present.

2) *They speak of God as permitting rather than willing evil.* Although evil is not absolutely outside God's will, it is included only indirectly, by God's permission. Such approaches have helped many generations of believers grapple with these difficult issues. They have not completely solved the problem, however, and the dilemma referred to earlier continues to arise: If God is all-powerful and chooses to do nothing about evil and suffering in the world, then God is not a loving creator.

One recent attempt to deal with this question of God's power in relation to the existence of evil is the work of process philosophers and theologians. Process thought, so called because it sees all reality as in process or constant evolution, emphasizes the interrelatedness of everything, seeing the universe as a kind of organism in which each entity influences every other. God is no exception to these general principles, as God and the world mutually influence each other.

The British philosopher, Alfred North Whitehead, who stands at the head of the school of process thought, speaks of God as the great companion, the fellow sufferer who understands. In the age-old dilemma about God's power and love, process theologians emphasize that God is a loving God, even if this means that divine power in the world is limited. God cannot prevent all evil, since there are other free agents operating in this world. We can thus turn to God to be strengthened and comforted in our suffering. If we believe God sends us our suffering, it is much harder to turn to God for help. But when we acknowledge that there are some things God does not control, we are free to be angry at what is happening without worrying that we are being angry at God or defying God's will. In other words, God is on our side, angry with us at the unfairness and the injustice.

It has not been common in Christian theology to view God as fellow sufferer. God has rather been presented as supremely happy, independent of the world, concerned about but not affected by the sufferings of human beings. Whitehead argues that it is not only more faithful to the biblical description to regard God as the fellow sufferer who understands, but is also far more compatible with the experience of love. To love others is to care about them. To care about them is to be affected by what happens to them. The very nature of love demands an openness and vulnerability where there is real reciprocal influence, i.e., mutual enrichment or diminishment in the interaction. If one has not been affected and changed in some way by one's relationship to another, it has to be questioned whether one has really loved. And so if God loves human beings, Whitehead maintains, then God is genuinely affected by whether their lives go well or ill. From this emerges Whitehead's image of God as the great companion, the fellow sufferer who understands.

In addition, God is a God of hope, continually showing us how to bring some good out of the evil in the world. To make this point Whitehead speaks of God as the poet of the world, with tender patience leading it by the divine vision of truth, beauty, and goodness. God is not a poet in the sense of one who writes poems. God is a poet rather in the sense of one with a vision of beauty, who holds up that vision to others in the hope that they might be attracted by it. In Whitehead's view, this is the gentle, noncoercive way God works with the world. God has a vision of truth, beauty, and goodness for the world, and in various ways God continually presents that vision to us, with tender patience soliciting our response.

According to process thought, then, God's power is limited by the reality of freedom in the world. God is not present in our suffering as the one who sends it, but rather as one struggling with us to bring some good out of it. God is actively involved not only in our individual struggles, but in our collective struggles as well. God is forever creating new possibilities and making the best of everything, even what can only be described as "evil." This does not mean that evil is a good. It is not; but it may be used for good.

Christian feminist theologians like Elizabeth Johnson and Dorothee Soelle also propose a new understanding of the relationship between divine power and love, their work often done in dialogue with process thought. Feminist theologians seek to heal whatever undermines the equality of women and men as made in the image and likeness of God. This means honoring women's experience as well as men's as a basis for theological reflection. Drawing on the experience of women, feminist theologians question a description of divine perfection in which God is not genuinely related to the world or affected by its suffering. Women's way of being in the world is grounded in connections. Absence of relationship signifies, not perfection, but the lack of something. Further, the notion of total power which is applied to God places too high a value on the traditionally male values of domination and control. From a feminist viewpoint, the idea that God permits great suffering while remaining unaffected is not acceptable.

They speak instead of a compassionate God who suffers in solidarity with the pain of the world. God does not suffer because of some deficiency, but out of the freedom of a love deliberately and generously shared. Compassionate love is thus not an imperfection but the highest excellence.

Passages of scripture support the idea of a suffering God. The prophet Isaiah offers the metaphor of a woman giving birth as a way of imagining the divine struggle to birth a new people and a new heaven and earth (Is 42:14). Delivery will only be complete in the future; until then, human beings are in solidarity with God in the birthing process. Other passages speak of the divine compassion. The book of Judges says that God hears the cry of the poor and is "moved to pity by their groanings because of those who afflicted and oppressed them" (Jgs 2:18). The voice Moses hears from the burning bush in Exodus indicates that God is well aware of what the people are suffering (Ex 3:7-8).

Feminist theologians also speak of God's power in a new way. Like process theologians, they resist dividing power and love from one another, so that love lacks power and power demands setting love aside. Sallie McFague sees the power of love operating by persuasion, care, attention, passion, and mutuality. Anne Carr describes power as respect for the freedom of others, as gentle persuasion, as patient love and encouragement, and notes that these are themes found in biblical descriptions of God. Feminist theologians therefore see divine power not as domineering or controlling, but as the liberating power of caring connectedness. God's compassionate love is present to the pain of the world to transform it from within. Such an explanation does not solve the mystery of suffering and evil or explain it away. Nor does it solve the mystery of God. What it gives us is a wellspring of hope to draw on as we join the struggle against evil.

A Contemporary Jewish Approach

Efforts to respond to tragedies like the death of a loved one or the progress of a disease involve not only dealing with the suffering itself, but, more importantly, finding some meaning in it. Many believers have found this meaning by being able to say in some way that it was God's will, or sent to them by God for a purpose. As we have seen, such statements create problems of their own.

In his best-selling book, *When Bad Things Happen to Good People*, Rabbi Harold Kushner develops many of the same points made by process thinkers, and, based on his experience of his son's tragic death, suggests that we rephrase our questions. We expend great efforts on the question, How could this happen? A better question is, Where does it lead? In other words, How will we respond?. What do we intend to do with life now? The challenge is to turn our pain from pointless suffering into an experience with meaning. While we may not be able to control the forces that cause our suffering, we can determine what the suffering will do to us. As a proverb puts it, "We cannot direct the wind, but we can adjust our sails." Rabbi Kushner also directs our attention to the frequently neglected fact that goodness, not evil, is the larger reality in life. That is why suffering and evil stand out.

We have summarized some of the common approaches to the problem of suffering and evil. These provide background for our next section in which we discuss the gospel perspective on these problems.

JESUS AND THE PROBLEM OF SUFFERING AND EVIL

If we turn to the gospels expecting an explanation for the existence of suffering and evil in the world, we will be disappointed. Jesus does not speculate on the reasons for suffering, nor does he provide rational, metaphysical solutions to it. He does not try to justify its existence in relation to God; nor does he gloss over it. In the gospels, suffering remains one of the great mysteries of human life.

Jesus is more concerned to show us how we are to respond. His approach is practical. In Jesus, God enters into our circumstances, feels what we feel, walks with us, and shows us what to do: 1) Jesus forgives sins and calls people to conversion; 2) Jesus heals; 3) Jesus conquers suffering and death in his resurrection; and 4) Jesus asks his disciples to carry on his struggle against sin and evil in the world.

Jesus Forgives Sins and Calls People to Conversion

When Jesus submits to suffering and death out of love for his fellow humans, he does not allow evil to destroy his fidelity to God nor his love for others. In other words, he refuses to continue the cycle of vengeance, to return evil for evil. He recognizes how much of the suffering and evil in the world is caused by the hatred allowed to grow in human hearts. Jesus reveals that it is love which breaks this power of human destruction. Because of the presence of his Spirit, this power continues to work within the community of his followers.

Knowing how much pain is caused by human moral failures, Jesus reduces this suffering by forgiving sins and calling people to conversion. Forgiveness of sin is central to Jesus' response to evil. He associates with sinners and calls them to repentance. The story of Zacchaeus in Luke's gospel (19:5-10) captures this aspect of Jesus' ministry. Zacchaeus is a senior tax collector and a wealthy man, but apparently too short to see Jesus above the crowds pressing to hear him. Anxious to catch a glimpse of Jesus, he climbs a sycamore tree. When Jesus reaches the tree, he looks up and says to him: "Zacchaeus, come down. Hurry, because I must stay at your house today." Zacchaeus welcomes Jesus joyfully, but those who are standing by complain because Jesus is going to stay at a sinner's house. Zacchaeus says to Jesus: "Look, sir, I am going to give half my property to the poor, and if I have cheated anybody I will pay him back four times the amount." Jesus replies, "Today salvation has come to this house, because this man too is a son of Abraham, for the Son of Man has come to seek out and save what was lost."

If we all started living the gospel, and stopped doing to ourselves and other creatures the harmful things we now so readily do, suffering and evil would be reduced tremendously. That is Jesus' vision of the reign of God.

Jesus Heals

Jesus appears in the gospels as the person in whom the reign of God breaks into the world, pushing back the powers of sin and death. When the kingdom comes in its fullness evil will be eliminated entirely. In his ministry Jesus works to heal people from their physical disabilities, their fears, their oppression, and their hunger. In doing so, he reveals God as near, as involved in human life.

Jesus' healing flows from his compassion. Compassion

means to suffer with someone, and the gospels show us that Jesus is with people in their pain. When his enemies ask him, "Why do you eat and drink with tax collectors and sinners?" Jesus answers them, "It is not those who are well who need the doctor, but the sick" (Lk 5:31). He is moved by the distress of a widow who has lost her son, by the suffering of people who are blind or paralyzed. People do not have to do anything special, or meet any requirements, to qualify for Jesus' compassion. He takes the suffering of others upon himself, and he expects his followers to do the same. No solution to the problem of suffering can bypass this demand. In Jesus we see the fullness of suffering love. Here both power and love take on new meaning. In Jesus we see God not absent from our suffering but actively at work to bring good out of it. Nearly one-fifth of the gospel is devoted to Jesus' healing. If it is God's action to heal disease, it can hardly be God's action to "send" that disease, either to punish or to discipline.

For a number of centuries, the healing aspect of Jesus' ministry was considered a thing of the past. People in those times were more naive, it was argued; they had little medical, scientific, and psychological sophistication. Various methods were used to explain away or account for the healings. The climate toward healing is changing, however. Many in the medical and scientific communities are recognizing the limits of their knowledge and skill in healing. There is readier acknowledgement that people need healing of many kinds—physical, psychological, spiritual, including the healing of memories—and that religious healing plays an important role in the human quest for wholeness. The ministry of healing is not something belonging to earlier times, but is an ongoing part of the Christian response to suffering and evil in the world. The attentive listening of a friend soothes a troubled heart. Painful memories are healed as individuals revisit traumatic events of the past with Jesus, are comforted, and feel empowered to let go of shame and bitterness. Christian communities lay hands and pray that individual members be healed of all that afflicts them. This ministry grows and shows great fruitfulness today.

Jesus Conquers Suffering and Death in His Resurrection

The healings we know in this life are all partial healings. However, they carry the promise of a more complete victory over suffering and evil. In fact, the most important thing Jesus offers in the face of suffering is hope of final victory. The central message of the gospel is the promise that death is not the last word; life is. Suffering is not the final reality; healing and resurrection are. The lives of Jesus' disciples are no longer dominated by the fear of death, but by the expectation of life. This is the mystery revealed in Jesus' death and resurrection.

The book of Genesis describes the entry of sin and evil into creation as a gradual breakdown of relationships (Gen 3). Women and men become alienated from their own bodies and feel shame at being naked; their relationship with one another and with the earth is characterized by domination and submission. Like a stone dropped into a pond of water, the circles of sin and hatred grow wider until brother kills brother in the story of Cain and Abel (Gen 4). In his life, death, and resurrection Jesus restores the lost harmony of relationships. Salvation in Jesus is called a new creation or reconciliation, for it reverses the effect of sin and joins people together again. Paul develops this theme in his letters to the Corinthians and Romans. We once were enemies, he says, but in Christ we are reconciled, made friends with God and one another (Rom 5:10-11; 2 Cor 5:18-19).

Suffering and Discipleship

Jesus neither praises suffering nor affirms that it is good. It is part of the reign of sin and death which he comes to heal. Therefore Jesus does not romanticize suffering as some streams of Christian spirituality have done; there is in the gospels no cult of pain and suffering for their own sake. Jesus' disciples are not instructed to seek suffering. They are told that if they remain disciples they will meet suffering and pain in carrying out their commitment, and they are not to let the risk of suffering divert them from this commitment. Jesus gives his life as an example, choosing toil and self-sacrifice, finally even accepting an unjust death, rather than turn from his mission.

As disciples of Jesus we cannot remain indifferent to the suffering which we see. The great test recounted in Matthew's gospel is based on what we have done or failed to do to alleviate the suffering of others:

> "Then the King will say to those on his right hand,
> 'Come, you whom my Father has blessed, take for your
> heritage the kingdom prepared for you since the
> foundation of the world. For I was hungry and you gave
> me food; I was thirsty and you gave me drink; I was a
> stranger and you made me welcome; naked and you
> clothed me, sick and you visited me, in prison and you
> came to me'" (Mt 25:34-37).

It is not enough that we do not inflict suffering on others. The call is to take action against suffering when we encounter it. Even though we cannot create a world entirely free from suffering and evil, we are expected to struggle against it as far as we can. We do not despair at its existence, but commit ourselves to battle against it as Jesus did. We too must heal, teach, console, assist, encourage—and try to change the structures that inflict suffering.

SUMMARY

One of the strongest challenges to Christian faith is the existence of suffering and evil in the world. Thinkers of every age have struggled to explain how a loving God could allow such evil. Contemporary explanations focus on the existence of created freedom as a limitation of God's power. They also point to the intrinsic connection between love and suffering, and the meaning of divine compassion. God freely chooses to create a free world and therefore cannot prevent all evil, but God is compassionate love, a source of hope and power, helping us to bring whatever good is possible out of evil.

Jesus' response to the mystery of suffering and evil takes place on the practical level. He reveals that God is a God of compassion. He forgives sin and calls people to conversion, thereby reducing the suffering in the world. He heals and sends his disciples to heal in his name. His death and resurrection promise a future victory over suffering and death, and inspire all Christians to engage in the struggle against evil in all its forms.

Questions and Exercises

1. What is the challenge which the existence of suffering and evil poses for belief in God?

2. In what areas of life is it most difficult for you to reconcile the power and love of God with the existence of suffering and evil?

3. What explanations do Job's friends give for his suffering? Recall some of the religious explanations for human suffering you have been given or those you have used to try to help others. Have these explanations eased the problem for you?

4. Briefly explain some of the biblical, classical, process, and feminist approaches to the problem of suffering and evil. Which do you find most convincing and least convincing? Why?

5. Describe Jesus' approach to the problem of suffering and evil. Do you find it compelling or disappointing?

6. List the attitudes and actions which should characterize the way a disciple of Jesus responds to the problem of suffering and evil.

7. Collect some stories of people who have found that the Christian message enabled them to create new meaning out of tragic events.

Suggestions for Further Reading

John B. Cobb, Jr. and David Ray Griffin, *Process Theology: An Introductory Exposition* (Westminster, 1975). One of the most helpful introductions to the process view of reality and its treatment of suffering and evil.

Wendy Farley, *Tragic Vision and Divine Compassion: A Contemporary Theodicy* (Westminster, 1990). Focuses the problem of evil on suffering rather than sin, and proposes compassion rather than punishment as the major form of God's power in relation to the world.

Wilfred Harrington, *The Tears of God: Our Benevolent Creator and Human Suffering* (The Liturgical Press, 1992). A scripture scholar offers a brief statement on how the bible strongly suggests a God who grieves, laments, and suffers.

Michael L. Peterson, ed., *The Problem of Evil: Selected Writings* (University of Notre Dame, 1992). Contains classical and contemporary pieces which reflect a broad range of approaches to the question of evil, as well as an extensive bibliography.

Lucien Richard, *What Are They Saying About the Theology of Suffering?* (Paulist, 1992). Surveys the theology of seven major contemporary thinkers and analyzes the diversity among their theologies of suffering.

Emilie M. Townes, ed., *A Troubling in My Soul: Womanist Perspectives on Evil and Suffering* (Orbis, 1993). Draws on black women's experience and literature to show the significance of the theme of God's relationship to suffering and evil in their lives.

Peter Vardy, *The Puzzle of Evil* (HarperCollins, 1992). Draws on the work of both secular and Christian writers to explore diverse responses to Christian belief in the face of evil.

Richard F. Vieth, *Holy Power, Human Pain* (Meyer-Stone, 1988). Reflects on the traditional problem of evil as it is confronted in our time and explores the resources of faith for healing human suffering.

CHAPTER 8

Christian Existence

What kind of life gives a sense of fulfillment? How do I find happiness? Is it the perfect body, the right degree, fashionable attire, the mate of my dreams, the big house, travel to exotic places? Keen interest in this question characterizes our age, but it is really just the most recent chapter in the ageless human quest for meaning and happiness. What is life really all about? How do we find peace, purpose, fulfillment?

Christians are supposed to learn the path to life from Jesus. But sometimes his teachings and example seem a thing of the past rather than a relevant dimension of life today. Our age, like every age, needs fresh examples to awaken the power and appeal of the gospel. Moved as we are much more by concrete embodiment than by general principles, we need stories to show us how Christian ideals can come to life in the flesh and blood of contemporary women and men.

Fortunately, compelling witnesses to the truth and beauty of the Christian vision do arise in each era. History reveals many different expressions of discipleship: the early martyrs, medieval cloistered religious, twentieth-century lay Christians. The effort to live out Christ's ideal in each new age produces individuals like Francis of Assisi, who in the twelfth century tries fully to embody Jesus' words about possessions and the poor; and Catherine of Siena, who

132

combines contemplation with politics amid the turmoil of the fourteenth century. By the power of their lives these individuals show us how to live Jesus' vision creatively and with new understanding. Often their lives stand in stark contrast to cultural images of the successful and fulfilled woman or man.

We reflect in this chapter on four Christians whose lives answer the question of Christian discipleship in our own time: Dietrich Bonhoeffer, Dorothy Day, Thomas Merton, and Fannie Lou Hamer. They come to understand Jesus' teaching by living it with all the risks and uncertainties that implies. As we follow their stories we begin to see that Christian existence can assume many forms in the same historical period. Even the journey of one person takes many turns. Christian life is not so much a single path as a series of choices in response to the call of the Spirit. We are called to find our true selves, and those selves keep evolving.

DIETRICH BONHOEFFER

In the German town of Flossenbürg is a tablet with the following inscription:

DIETRICH BONHOEFFER, A WITNESS OF JESUS CHRIST AMONG HIS BRETHREN. BORN FEB. 4, 1906, IN BRESLAU. DIED APRIL 9, 1945, IN FLOSSENBÜRG.

Bonhoeffer was executed in a Nazi prison camp at the age of 39.

Bonhoeffer's life might easily have taken a different course. He grows up with every advantage, a brilliant son in a wealthy household. He and his twin sister, Sabine, are the sixth and seventh children in a tightly knit family. A fine athlete, Dietrich plays tennis expertly and swims often and well. His father is an agnostic; his brothers choose prestigious careers in law and research. Bonhoeffer enters the ministry.

Even this choice need not dramatically alter the direction of his life. He excels in his university studies and fits easily into the structures of the Lutheran Church he wishes to serve. However, events in Germany gradually challenge his commitment to Christ and force him into the agonies of choice.

In 1935, disappointed by his official church's refusal to take a stand against the policies of Hitler, Bonhoeffer takes over leadership of the seminary of the German Confessing Church. As this Finkenwalde seminary is forced more and more underground and finally boarded up by the Hitler regime, Bonhoeffer writes in his book, *The Cost of Discipleship*: "How do I live a Christian life in the world? What does it mean to be a disciple of Jesus Christ?" The demands of discipleship are unconditional, Bonhoeffer concludes. There is no "cheap grace," for discipleship is participation in Christ's suffering for others. It means following in the footsteps of Christ who is the "man for others."

Although he has at first preached no politics, Bonhoeffer now becomes active in political affairs and the resistance against Hitler. He travels extensively, using his ecumenical contacts to win support outside Germany for the resistance movement. In June of 1939 friends arrange for a trip to New York City, but by early July Bonhoeffer is sailing back to Germany. In a letter to a friend he explains his decision. He will have no right, he says, to participate in rebuilding Christian life in Germany after the war if he does not share this time of trial with his people. German Christians are facing the terrible alternative of either willing the defeat of their own nation so that Christian civilization can survive, or willing the victory of their nation and with it the destruction of civilization. Bonhoeffer knows which alternative he must choose, and he realizes it means the loss of all security.

A pacifist, and nonviolent by nature, Bonhoeffer has long wanted to visit Gandhi in India to learn more about his nonviolent methods. Three different times he must cancel plans for such a visit. Now, back in Germany, he gradually moves from pacifism to direct political action. In a momentous ethical decision, he becomes a participant in a plot to assassinate Hitler. If a madman is driving a motorcar in a crowded street, he says, it is not only my task to look after the victims of the madman. I must do all in my power to stop his driving at all.

On January 17, 1943, Bonhoeffer becomes engaged to Maria von Wedemeyer. On April 5 of that year his house is searched and he is arrested and placed in Tegal prison.

His letters from prison frequently mention his delight in the beauty and mystery of little things—a thrush, an anthill, chestnut and lime trees. Bonhoeffer believes that the Ultimate or Transcendent is found in this world, in this life with one another. Christ must be found at the center, not at the edges of our existence. Bonhoeffer is convinced that it is only by living completely in the world that one learns to have faith. But his decisions do not come easily. Bonhoeffer keenly feels his weaknesses and his longings. In a poem entitled "Who Am I?" written toward the end of his prison stay, he muses on people's comments that he is calm, cheerful, and friendly in spite of his confinement. But he asks:

> Am I then really all that which other people tell of?
> Or am I only what I know of myself,
> restless and longing and sick,
> like a bird in a cage, struggling for breath, as though
>   hands were compressing my throat,
> yearning for colours, for flowers, for the voices of birds,
> thirsting for words of kindness, for neighbourliness,

trembling with anger at despotisms and petty humiliation,
tossing in expectation of great events,
powerlessly trembling for friends at an infinite distance,
weary and empty at praying, at thinking, at making,
faint, and ready to say farewell to it all?

His struggle ends on the spring dawn of April 9, 1945.
Bonhoeffer has been moved from his Tegal prison to
Buchenwald concentration camp and then to Flossenbürg.
He is asked to hold a morning service for the other prisoners.
He reads and prays the texts for the day:

"With his stripes we are healed" (Isa 53:5).

"Blessed be the God and Father of our Lord Jesus
Christ! By God's great mercy we have been born anew
to a living hope through the resurrection of Jesus Christ
from the dead" (1 Pet 1:3).

After the service other prisoners want to smuggle him over to
their room so that he can hold a service there also. But the
door opens and a voice calls out: "Prisoner Bonhoeffer, get
ready and come with us!" And on that grey Monday morning,
he is hanged.

DOROTHY DAY

When Dorothy Day dies in 1980 at the age of eighty-
three, historian David O'Brien, in a *Commonweal* article, calls
her "the most significant, interesting, and influential person
in the history of American Catholicism." Her own goal for
the Catholic Worker movement, which she founds, is much
more modest. Its declared purpose is to realize in the individual and in society the teachings of Christ.

Dorothy grows up in a warm, affectionate family, and
throughout her life she reads avidly: the bible, Shakespeare,

Upton Sinclair, Dostoevsky, Tolstoy. The words of Jesus and his early disciples fit her vision of how the world should be, but when she looks for Christians, she sees that they are like everybody else. She does not, she says, see anyone having a banquet and calling in the lame, the halt and the blind (Lk 14). She wants everyone really to love one another, and this longing for community and solidarity leads her, in her first year of college, to join the socialist party.

When she is twenty-four, she and her lover Forster Batterham establish a rickety household on the Staten Island shore. "The man I loved, with whom I entered into a common law marriage," she writes later in her autobiography, *The Long Loneliness*, "was an anarchist, an Englishman by descent, and a biologist." Dorothy conceives a child, and it is this child, she says, that causes her faith to mature. When Tamar is born, she has to be baptized. Tamar's baptism and her own baptism in the church mean that Dorothy has to leave Forster who is irrevocably opposed to religion. Dorothy has spent her youth among socialists and anarchists, and in their view she has gone over to the church of wealth and power. But Dorothy believes that, for all its sins, it is also the church of the poor and dispossessed.

In 1932, having been a rather aimless Catholic for five years, Dorothy begins to wonder whether Christianity is so old it has become stale. She visits the national shrine at the Catholic University and prays that some way will open up for her to use her talents for the poor. Upon her return to New York she meets Peter Maurin, with whom she founds the Catholic Worker. At the end of *The Long Loneliness* Dorothy describes the Catholic Worker beginnings by saying that she and her friends were just sitting around talking when lines of people formed saying, "We need bread." How could they tell them, "Go, and be filled"? They had to share what they had.

The Houses of Hospitality do, in fact, develop without

much advance planning. At the New York Catholic Worker building on Charles Street, for instance, there is always coffee and a pot of soup on the stove, and anyone who comes to the door is welcome to share a meal. As word gets around, hundreds begin lining up at the door each day. By the time Dorothy dies this sharing of bread has led to a network of some fifty communities across the country. These Houses of Hospitality have sheltered thousands and served millions of meals. Hospitality, Dorothy believes, means more than giving the poor a meal or bed. It means opening our hearts to their needs. Jesus himself walked among the poor and experienced exile and the life of a wanderer. We cannot hope to know him unless we turn to our needy neighbors in love.

Dorothy's is not the kind of holiness that fits easily into pious books on the saints. "Don't call me a saint," she says. "I don't want to be dismissed that easily." Dorothy is strong-willed and independent. She can hold a grudge and explode with anger. When people at hospitality houses steal her books, she finds it hard to contain her rage. Once when someone cautions her in a heated moment to hold her temper, she replies, "I hold more temper in one minute than you will in your entire life." She resents others' curiosity about her; she is reticent and dislikes political confrontation. She keeps on loving the poor, but she hates the lice they bring with them.

Dorothy is a pacifist. She does not believe that violence or war, any kind of war, can be reconciled with the gospel. She maintains this stand during American reactions to the Civil War in Spain, World War II, and the war in Vietnam. In the 1950s, with the construction of the hydrogen bomb, atmospheric testing, and civil defense drills, she receives several jail terms of up to thirty days for her refusal to cooperate with New York City's compulsory civil defense drills. Dorothy is convinced that the works of mercy cannot be separated from the works of peace. Christians are to feed the hungry, but war destroys crops and brings starvation. Christians are to comfort the afflicted, but war brings misery and terror. She bases her belief on Christ's relentless insistence on the way of love: "Love your enemies, do good to those who persecute you" (Mt 5:44). Jesus substituted the cross for the sword or bomb as the instrument of justice.

With all of her concern about poverty and war, Dorothy never forgets life's joys and beauties. She meditates on scripture every day. In her columns for *The Catholic Worker* she frequently quotes Dostoevsky's words: "The world will be saved by beauty." If we fail to rejoice in the sun, the moon, the stars, in the cool breezes and rivers, we are, she says, contributing to life's misery. Her last writings are on these themes: the beauty of nature, the love and mercy of God, the need for forgiveness and celebration.

THOMAS MERTON

On December 9, 1941, Thomas Merton boards a train in freezing rain in Olean, New York, to begin his journey to a monastery in Gethsemani, Kentucky. He has decided to become a Trappist monk. In his best-selling autobiography, *Seven Storey Mountain*, Merton describes himself as a troubled youth who seeks peace in the monastic cloister and freedom from the enticements of the world.

The early years of Merton's life are, in fact, traumatic. First there is the loss of his mother, who dies when he is a child. His memories of their relationship leave him feeling inadequate and a failure, constantly measured against an unattainable standard. Then his father develops a brain tumor and dies when Thomas is sixteen; it is the greatest tragedy of his life. Ever after he longs for parents and a home.

Frequently he suffers loneliness. He yearns for love—but finds it difficult to accept when it is given.

Attractive and bright, Merton wins a scholarship to Cambridge University. But in the spring of 1934, fathering a child out of wedlock, he loses his scholarship, is disowned by his patron, and returns to America in disgrace. He attends Columbia University where he finds a circle of friends who remain important to him the rest of his life. Photographs of Merton in his Columbia days show him looking like a man-about-town. He drinks a good deal and spends evenings with his fraternity brothers in the speakeasies on 52nd Street. These friends are astounded when Merton becomes a Catholic and later joins the Trappists.

As Michael Mott details in his biography, *The Seven Mountains of Thomas Merton*, Merton wrestles within himself with the difficult spiritual conflicts of his time: Should I involve myself in the struggle of the world for its fulfillment, or withdraw from all worldly concerns and seek God alone? Should I enjoy my sexuality to the full, marry and settle down, or renounce sexuality entirely and concentrate on developing my inner life alone? How can I enjoy or even seek peace and serenity when so many people everywhere are suffering? What sense does it make to submit myself to the petty horizons of religious superiors when Christ calls us to the liberty of the children of God? In all his questions, Merton's anchor is the life of prayer, which he describes in a letter to a Muslim as being centered entirely on attention to God's presence, will, and love. One of his constant pleasures is reading the scriptures. They fill his mind with rich images. Andrew, Peter, James and John were human like us, Merton reflects, and like them we bring our infirmities to Christ in order that his strength may transform our weakness. We feel Christ's eyes upon us as we sit under the fig tree, and our souls stir to life.

During his years at Gethsemani Merton suffers periods of disillusionment with monastic life. More than once he finds himself at odds with the abbot and many of his brothers. Among other things, he has a passion for writing, which depends in turn on extensive reading. But there is no precedent for this in Trappist life, and Merton many times experiences anguished self-doubt when his life as a writer is called into question by his community. But he persists, with grudging leave, and by the time of his death has published sixty books and hundreds of articles and prefaces. His commitment to writing, added to the other demands of Trappist life, leads many times to overwork and exhaustion, sometimes to near collapse.

In the 1960s Merton begins a period of growing involvement with the world's suffering, which contrasts with his early years at Gethsemani when he had seen his goal as one of total detachment from the world. He is now convinced that Christian commitment means choosing the world, in the sense of faithfully doing the work one is capable of doing to make the world more free, just, livable, and human. Merton begins to grapple with the terrible possibilities of nuclear war. During ecumenical meetings at Gethsemani in 1963, he describes the Christian's duty in the face of nuclear war as one of striving in every way to protect and preserve God's creation and to save humanity for which Christ died.

From his Trappist hermitage Merton becomes a leader in the peace movement, and many who share his views write to him or come to see him. His concern with the plight of the Latin American poor also grows. This awareness begins during the two years when the Nicaraguan poet Ernesto Cardenal is a novice under Merton. The two continue to correspond, and Merton considers himself to be in deep communion with the forces of life and hope struggling for the renewal of Latin America.

Merton's many writings on prayer reach countless people. During his twenty-seven years in the monastery, he comes to see monks as not very different from other people. They should not be supposed heroic or saintly, he says. They wrestle with the same problems other people do, but try to get to the spiritual roots of them. People lose happiness, Merton writes, because they forget how to experience their spiritual selves and therefore cannot be whole or free. In prayer we become aware of our real selves, and in so doing realize that we must live for others and, above all, for God. True identity, Merton believes, comes from contemplation, and in this the Christian is a sign of hope for a world suffering from estrangement and inauthentic selfhood.

Merton's life ends in the Orient, where the great religions of the world began. His interest in the east goes back to his early years. He has long been interested in Zen Buddhism, and is convinced that Christians, and especially monks, can improve the quality of their lives by making contact with Buddhism or Hinduism. Some of the books that mean the most to him are his reflections on the relationship of Zen to Christianity, *Mystics and Zen Masters* and *Zen and the Birds of Appetite*. In December 1968 he is in Bangkok to speak at a conference on monastic renewal organized by an international Benedictine group. Merton concludes his talk with a plea for Christian openness to other religions, other ways of life, and above all to the painfulness of inner change. After his talk he goes to his room for a siesta. He is found dead at the end of the afternoon rest period, an electric fan lying across his chest.

It is not clear how Merton has died; it may have been a heart attack or a fatal electric shock. Great and poignant as this loss is to many, it is in a way fitting that he die here. His Asian journey is the culmination of years of study of the east. He feels a growing need to harness all the spiritual energies available to humankind in the interest of saving the world. He listens and learns from many of the Buddhist and Hindu teachers he meets in Asia, finding in them holiness and a deep knowledge of prayer. They, in turn, recognize in him an authentic Buddha.

FANNIE LOU HAMER

Her name is less familiar than those of Dietrich Bonhoeffer, Thomas Merton, and Dorothy Day, but it should not be. Fannie Lou Hamer is one of the great women of the black freedom struggle and a beacon of hope for many.

Born in 1917 into a family of black sharecroppers in the Mississippi Delta, Fannie Lou grows up as the youngest of 20 children. One of the poorest regions of the poorest state in the union, the Delta depends for its economic base on cotton grown on large plantations. A white minority control the political power and all the wealth. Blacks are reminded of their place by the detailed Jim Crow code which segregates or reserves for whites-only all public facilities, including cafes, bus stations, and movie theaters. A complex literary test which only blacks have to take and a poll tax keep blacks from voting.

At one point, through relentless hard work, the Hamer family is able to rent some land outright. They buy animals and equipment and fix up a home. But their dreams are crushed and they are forced back into sharecropping when a white man poisons the feed and kills their stock. After marrying and adopting two daughters, Fannie Lou and her family continue to work for twenty years on various plantations around Sunflower County. While picking cotton, she sometimes says to those working with her: "Hard as we work for nothing, there must be some way we can change things."

In 1962 Hamer attends a rally sponsored by the

Southern Christian Leadership Conference and the Student Nonviolent Coordinating Committee. The sermon at the rally is from Matthew 16:3. This verse is about "reading the signs of the times," and the preacher ties it to the problem of voter registration in Mississippi, where blacks are denied fundamental rights. A call goes out at the meeting for blacks to go to the county seat the next week and register. Fannie Lou, now forty-five, answers the call. As a result, she is evicted from her plantation home and the family property is subsequently confiscated by the owner. She is never again free from such persecution as she moves into full-time work in the civil rights movement.

At one point she and a group of workers are returning by bus from a voter education workshop in Charleston, South Carolina. When they arrive at the Trailways station in Winona and enter the white side of the terminal, they are arrested, held for three days, and brutally beaten. Hamer suffers permanent impairment of the vision in her left eye. In spite of the beatings, Hamer refuses to give in to hatred and revenge. It would not solve any problem, she says, for her to hate her enemies or any person: "I feel sorry for anybody that could let hate wrap them up. Ain't no such thing as I can hate anybody and hope to see God's face."

Throughout her life, Fannie Lou Hamer remains firmly rooted in biblical faith. She does not think of herself as a great historical leader, but as someone simply carrying out the gospel injunction to tend the sick and bring liberty to the captives. The passage she uses most at freedom meetings is from Luke's gospel:

> The spirit of the Lord has been given to me,
> for God
> has anointed me,
> sending me to bring good news to the poor,
> to proclaim liberty to captives

and to the blind new sight,
to set the downtrodden free,
and to proclaim the year of God's favour (Lk 4:18-19).

Prayer and optimism sustain Hamer, and she refuses to categorize people as good or bad. There is some good in the worst people, she insists, and some bad in the best. She wants us to keep looking for the good. Hamer is convinced that Christianity means being concerned about our fellow human beings.

A university student who goes south with other volunteers during the 1964 Freedom Summer campaigns remembers most of all the inspiration Fannie Lou provides through her singing. She puts new words to old songs of faith like "This Little Light":

This little light of mine, I'm gonna let it shine...
    Let it shine, let it shine, let it shine!
Jesus gave it to me now, I'm gonna let it shine...
I've got the light of freedom, I'm gonna let it shine...
All over the Delta, I'm gonna let it shine...
    Let it shine, let it shine, let it shine!

Across the United States and in one trip to West Africa, Fannie Lou Hamer carries her message for fifteen years. She struggles not only against racism, but against war; she promotes women's rights and organizes antipoverty and economic self-help efforts. She dies in 1977 after a long bout with cancer, and is buried in a Sunflower County cotton field, on black cooperative farm land.

SUMMARY

We have looked briefly at the lives of four Christians from our own era. None of them was perfect. Neither were the saints of the past. Their Christian commitment did not eliminate limitations and failings. But even in these brief sketches, we can see something of the heart of Christian existence. Two characteristics stand out. The first is reliance on God. Nourished by a life of prayer, trust in God helps the Christian overcome fear, and produces independence, courage, and freedom in the Spirit.

Secondly, Christian existence is characterized by love and service to others, helping to establish the reign of God in the world. Christians are prepared to give up possessions, prestige, power, and even life for the same reason Jesus was willing to do so, out of love and concern for others. In our present cultural context, marked as it is by such disparity between rich and poor and by the oppression of racism, sexism, and militarism, the commitment to Christian love frequently takes the form of public action. Christians believe that goodness can overcome evil, and they work to make Jesus' vision actual. This work gradually draws them into the death/resurrection mystery.

Christian existence is not external imitation of Jesus. It flows from inner conversion, and is a matter of the spirit and the heart. No two Christian lives will be exactly the same in their externals. Some marry; some do not. Some live relatively quiet lives; others are at the center of publicity. The persons whose lives we have explored felt called upon to live out the gospel in public and heroic ways. Others live their call in ordinary experiences of friendship, family life, or work. Whatever the difference in details, Christian existence will always be a life centered on love of God and neighbor as Jesus' life was.

Questions and Exercises

1. Why is it important that the life and message of Jesus be embodied in new ways in each historical period?

2. What are some of our culture's dominant images of human fulfillment and happiness? In what ways do the lives presented here stand in contrast to them?

3. What similarities and differences do you find in the way these four individuals provide an answer to Bonhoeffer's question: How do I live a Christian life in the world?

4. All of the Christians discussed in this chapter applied Jesus' teaching to social issues. Is this an essential aspect of the gospel message?

5. See yourself as a pilgrim traveling through this century. List the most important contribution each of these lives might make to your journey.

6. Briefly describe the lives of other Christians, well known or not so well known, who have modeled Christian existence for you.

Suggestions for Further Reading

Eberhard Bethge, *Costly Grace* (Harper, 1979). An illustrated introduction which presents a compelling portrait of Dietrich Bonhoeffer.

Frederick Buechner, *The Sacred Journey* (Harper & Row, 1982). A writer of fiction and non-fiction reflects on the key moments of the first half of his life, discovering how God's words unfold in a myriad different ways.

Robert Ellsberg, ed., *By Little and By Little: The Selected Writings of Dorothy Day* (Alfred A. Knopf, 1983). Selections from her books, articles, and columns, accompanied by a fine introduction to her life.

Monica Furlong, *Merton: A Biography* (Harper and Row, 1980). Presents Merton as one who understood and revealed much about the role of religion in the twentieth century.

Renny Golden, *The Hour of the Poor, The Hour of Women: Salvadoran Women Speak* (Crossroad, 1991). Stories of twelve living and three martyred El Salvadoran women whose Christian faith is shaped by service to their people and the violence that accompanies it.

James McClendon, *Biography as Theology: How Life Stories Can Remake Today's Theology*. Revised edition (Trinity Press International, 1990). Shows the importance of significant individuals like Martin Luther King and Dag Hammarskjöld in shaping the Christian community.

Letty Russell, Kwok Pui-lan, Ada María Isasi-Díaz, and Katie Geneva Canon, eds., *Inheriting Our Mothers' Gardens: Feminist Theology in Third World Perspective* (Westminster, 1988). Eight life stories by women from different backgrounds illustrating the historical and social dimensions of their shared Christian faith.

CHAPTER 9

The Church

The well-known evangelical theologian, Jim Wallis, founder of the Sojourners Community in Washington, D.C., says that when he was a university student he was unsuccessfully evangelized by almost every Christian group on campus. His basic response to their preaching was, "How can I believe when I look at the way the church lives?" They replied, "Don't look at the church. Look at Jesus."

Many who admire the life and teachings of Jesus echo Wallis' sentiments. They find it easier to believe in Jesus than to accept the churches that bear his name. In the United States today there is heightened interest in religion, prayer, and transcendent experience. The majority of people say they believe in God and in life after death. Many are drawn to a personal relationship with Jesus, and interest in the bible is high. But the attraction to Jesus contrasts with lack of interest in the church. Today, perhaps more than ever, there are Christians outside the church, outside all the churches. Mohandas Gandhi loved Jesus. A house guest of Gandhi's in 1942 noticed the one decoration on the mud walls of his little hut: a black-and-white print of Jesus Christ under which was written, "He Is Our Peace." But Gandhi believed that much of what passes as Christianity is a negation of Jesus' sermon on the mount.

So alongside the question of faith in Jesus arises the

question, Why the church? Why should I remain in the church and involve myself actively in its life? If I do not belong to the church, why should I join? With such questions in mind, this chapter examines five aspects of the relationship between Jesus and the church: 1) Jesus and the founding of the church; 2) Christian faith and life in community; 3) the church as institution; 4) the church as a community of disciples; and 5) the church's mission.

We speak here of church in the sense of those major denominations founded on belief in Jesus Christ. Since the Protestant reformation in the sixteenth century, western Christianity has been divided, and the different Christian churches have sometimes been locked in bitter conflict. Recognizing the scandal of such divisions, the various Christian denominations have, in recent decades, worked toward greater unity and understanding among themselves. The ecumenical movement demonstrates how fruitful it is for Christians respectfully to explore their differences. For the purposes of our chapter, therefore, we will be focusing on questions that relate to the existence of any Christian church at all, rather than on differences in doctrine and practice among existing churches.

JESUS AND THE FOUNDING OF THE CHURCH

One of the first questions usually asked is, Did Jesus found the church? If so, how? The response of the churches has generally been to emphasize that Jesus established the official structures of the church. For example, Roman Catholics have stressed that Jesus gave the "power of the keys" to Peter and through Peter to his successors called "the popes." The goal of such arguments is to show that Jesus intended a structured religious group to carry on his work after his death, and that he himself initiated the specifics of this structure: papacy, episcopacy, priesthood, sacraments. This attempt to show that aspects of the present church stand in direct relationship to the historical Jesus continues around issues such as the ordination of women, the number of official sacraments, and the exercise of authority in the church.

What is at stake here is not only the controversies between Roman Catholics and Protestants over what sort of church order was divinely willed. The question for Christians today is whether Jesus intended to found a church at all, and thus whether any church is a legitimate continuation of his vision and practice. In the early twentieth century, a German theologian, Adolf von Harnack, phrased this challenge in a way that shapes the modern problem: How could Jesus' imminent expectation of the last days allow for the church? In his book *What Is Christianity?* he states that the essence of Christianity is Jesus' message of the kingdom of God as the rule of God in the hearts of individuals. The church as an institution with its dogmas, hierarchy, and rituals does not belong to this essence. In the course of further discussions, this thesis gave birth to a popular slogan: "Jesus foretold the kingdom, and it was the church that came."

The relationship of Jesus to the church is a serious and important one for any Christian, and so the discussion of these issues has continued. Biblical scholarship of the past few decades has alerted us to the fact that asking if Jesus *intended* to found a church may not be the right question. Our biblical sources are not primarily interested in exploring Jesus' intentions, and do not enable us to answer that question with any certitude. However, several fruitful approaches to the question of Jesus' institution of the church have been explored and will be summarized here.

One approach sees the church as God's creation through the action of the Spirit. Jesus did not institute the church by formally establishing particular organizational structures, but by his death and resurrection and the sharing of his spirit of new life. While it is possible to find a basis for certain church structures in Jesus' actions, the earliest Christian communities did not see themselves as an organized religious group or as starting a new religious movement. What held them together was rather a shared faith experience, the salvation that had occurred in Jesus' death and resurrection. The basis of their unity was not structure and organization, but a common faith and life in Christ's spirit. The development of authority, leadership, law, and sacraments took place gradually as part of their effort to live and preserve that spirit.

A second way of expressing this relation between the church and Jesus is to emphasize the church's continuation of Jesus' vision. Do the preaching and actions of Jesus have a meaning that makes the emergence of the church legitimate? The early Christian communities express a strong conviction that Jesus is the source of the community's holiness and justice, and the center of the new reality of Christian life. Mark's gospel shows Jesus forming a new family of disciples rooted in the sharing of Jesus' suffering, disciples with a fresh set of values. Luke emphasizes the gradual emergence of the church as others follow in Jesus' footsteps and share their wealth with one another. In this way the early Christian communities expressed their belief that their foundation is in Christ. The Pauline writings draw out this relationship by speaking of the individual community as the body of Christ. The founding of the church, therefore, did not take place in one single institutional act but gradually, as Jesus' followers began through the Spirit to discover their own way and the implications of their calling. The relationship of the church to Jesus lies in its continuity with his vision and actions. In summary, there exists among scholars today a consensus that in one sense Jesus founded a church, in another he did not. Jesus did not directly begin a new religious organization, but he did lay the groundwork for one in many ways.

CHRISTIAN FAITH AND LIFE IN COMMUNITY

Another way to answer the question "Why the church?" is to look at what is required to live the life of faith. Conversion to Christ and persistence in the way of life it demands calls for an environment which makes the Christian life possible. Generally speaking, we do not believe in isolation; we believe in the context of a particular historical community, whether that community be a communist cell, a Benedictine monastery, or a Protestant congregation. We are formed from earliest life by communities, starting with our family, and our ways of seeing the world are profoundly shaped by the stories and images of our social groups. Without the church we would have no scriptures nor any sacraments, for the scriptures are a community book and the sacraments are the ritual actions of the community. In *Habits of the Heart*, sociologist Robert Bellah and other researchers report that, in spite of variations in doctrine and worship, most Protestant and Catholic local churches in the United States define themselves as communities of support.

We spoke earlier of a certain kind of doubt as intrinsic to the life of faith. The burden of this doubt can sometimes be too overwhelming for an individual believer to bear. A community is a place where doubt can be shared and addressed. Beliefs can also be tested in community. What we believe individually can be weighed against the memory and long history of a community, its tradition. In turn, our individual beliefs may be a prophetic voice calling the community to new life and growth, as was the case with Martin Luther and Dorothy Day.

A community also preserves the world of belief in its totality in a way no individual believer can. Not all the truths of revelation hold the same meaning for each person. Each believer and each epoch have truths that predominate and more forcefully shape the pattern of their life. Believers united in a community preserve and illumine the total Christian mystery for one another.

We need the support of a community to continue believing. Faith is at many points in tension with the cultures in which we live. Most faiths are held by a minority. Joining a faith and persevering in it require contact with mature Christians who represent Christ and the Christian way of life. These communities offer indispensable supports. Besides serving as living models, they often provide counseling and spiritual direction to their members, as well as material help in time of need. They usually also contain groups within the group—for bible study, prayer, and healing. They serve too as a locus of social life and celebration.

Recently a new movement has developed within the churches: base communities. These usually include the elements named but add another as essential: social criticism and action. Base communities in several countries of the world attempt to unite theological and biblical reflection with social analysis leading to action for justice. One such group in Italy, for example, after reflecting on passages from Exodus, saw a parallel between the biblical situation and the poverty in which many of their members lived, and determined to do something about it. We need community not only to persevere and grow in believing, but to have the insight and courage to take action as our faith compels us to.

THE CHURCH AS INSTITUTION

It is not too difficult to see that Christian faith requires the support of a community. What is harder to accept is the institutional shape of these communities in our day. In fact, community and institution are often equated and rejected by many as avenues of personal fulfillment. A stance that is becoming more common is to remain with the church but with profound indifference to its institutional life. Most Americans view the Catholic Church in particular as highly institutional. Their image of the church features hierarchical officials, dogmas, and laws most prominently, all of them demanding conformity. In earlier historical periods when people were accustomed to being ruled by others in many areas of their lives, such institutionalism was more readily accepted. Today, a critical view of all institutions predominates. People are unwilling to support the laws and dogmas of the church if they seem to control and crush the spirit rather than build up and nourish people of faith.

We are sometimes shocked to find sinfulness present in the churches. But Christian community is not a gathering of those already completely saved. It is the place where we open ourselves to forgiveness and further conversion. The church has sometimes mistakenly seen itself as a community of the saved. In a spirit of triumphalism it has confused itself with the reign of God. While on the way to the kingdom, the church remains a mixture of good and evil. This gives rise to the ambivalence we feel about the church as institution.

This ambivalence creates contrasting attitudes toward the institutional aspects of the church. There are, first of all, the positive aspects of the church's life, which attract many to it. They appreciate the beauty and tradition of 2000 years of Christian life. They are drawn to the power of the liturgy and the spirit of warmth found in many churches. They admire those church people who seem to stand firmly behind what they believe and bring the power of their churches to bear on current issues of social importance. The existence of certain dogmas and beliefs gives them a sense of security amid the confusing array of modern options. They want a clear and forceful stand on moral issues and the witness that many church leaders give on problems of world-wide scope. If there were no churches to speak out publicly and credibly on moral concerns they know we would all be impoverished.

On the other hand, the church is the object of widespread criticism. It is accused not only of being behind the times, but of falling far short of its mission. The Catholic Church especially is accused of making of its hierarchical institutions, doctrines, and laws ends in themselves, and of confusing personal opinions in high places with divine directives. Many women feel alienated from a church that does not recognize their experience and contributions, and denies them full participation. Non-practicing Christians young and old point to bad sermons, dull liturgies, authoritarian dogmas and narrow-minded moral theology. They are scandalized when the church sides with the powerful and wealthy at the expense of the oppressed and exploited. Throughout the centuries Christians have killed one another in the name of the Jesus who came to bring love on earth, and this too has led to disillusionment with institutionalized Christianity.

Whatever its attractions, noninstitutionalism is in reality impossible. Whenever beliefs are held by more than one person and sustained over time, they become institutionalized. Fresh attempts to create Christian communities in our era demonstrate this fact. Since human faith and community are never purely spiritual, they cannot escape certain rules and structures. However, establishment of these forms brings with it the danger of inflexibility. The Christian task is, therefore, continually to renew and reform the church so that it is what it is meant to be. That is why many have suggested images of the church which balance and offset the dangers of too much emphasis on the institution: the church rather as body of Christ, as mystical communion, as sacrament, as herald, as servant. One model that is gaining prominence today is the church as a community of disciples.

THE CHURCH AS COMMUNITY OF DISCIPLES

Roman Catholic theologian Avery Dulles has suggested that the most appropriate image of the church for our times is the church as a community of disciples. Discipleship does not mean simply imitating the historical Jesus. It means receiving and interpreting Jesus' meaning and significance anew in ever changing circumstances.

As Dulles points out, this image seems appropriate for the church for a number of reasons. First of all, it fits our contemporary experience of church. Christians are now a minority in nearly every country of the world. In such a situation they can more readily identify with the early church's understanding of itself as disciples or witnesses than with descriptions of the church in terms of triumph or power. Second, Christians who join the church or remain in it today are less likely to do so simply for cultural reasons. Like disciples, they must hear and respond freely to a personal call. Third, discipleship as described in the Christian scriptures is a precarious relationship, for it is possible to deny the Master, as did some of the first disciples. Viewing the church as a community of disciples reminds us that our relationship to Jesus is grounded in grace. Fourth, a disciple is not simply a passive consumer or critic. We are tempted to see the church as an institution over against us from which we receive things—teachings, sacraments, laws, grace—or whose faults we dislike. The image of the church as a community of disciples reminds us that we ourselves are the church, responsible for shaping its reality and for contributing to its life.

The image of discipleship presents a more modest notion of the church than some of the models used historically such as perfect society or people of God. A disciple is one who is on the way, but who has not yet arrived. To be a disciple is to be a learner, someone still struggling to comprehend strange words or unravel puzzling experiences. We see the disciple engaged in this learning throughout scripture. Life in the church is thus one of continual conversion. It means following Jesus in new and challenging circumstances, and supporting other followers of Jesus as they accept this call. Together we try to grow, often slowly and painfully.

Roman Catholic theologian Elisabeth Schüssler Fiorenza expands our understanding of the church as a community of disciples. In her book, *In Memory of Her*, Fiorenza shows that the Jesus movement of first-century Palestine created a discipleship of *equals*. In contrast to the Greco-Roman society of that time, the Christian community welcomed women as well as men into full discipleship, slave as well as free. Jesus ate and drank not only with women, but with sinners, prostitutes, beggars, tax collectors, the ritually unclean, the crippled, and the destitute. In the Christian community, differences must not evolve into patterns of dominance and submission. Rather, the all-inclusive goodness of God demands equality. Fiorenza challenges the church to return to Jesus' vision of a discipleship of equals.

THE CHURCH'S MISSION

When we ask the question "Why the church?" we are also asking about the role or purpose of the church in the world today. In the past the church's mission was sometimes seen primarily as making converts, increasing church membership. One major shift in understanding the church today is the conviction that the church does not exist only to be of service to itself. Though Jesus' message does fulfill our own deepest hopes and longings, it also compels us to be of service to the world around us. The church exists to nourish the spiritual life of its members so that they can work to establish the reign of God in the world: a transformed social order in which peace and justice prevail.

Pronouncements of the different churches today demonstrate the intrinsic link between work for justice and the preaching of the gospel. Human dignity and Christian love demand such action. Religion is concerned with the whole of life—with social, economic, and political matters as well as with private and personal ones. The church must therefore continually attempt to interpret "the signs of the times," as the Second Vatican Council said, in order to bring the vision of Jesus to life and show its application in each new era.

From the beginning Christians understood the message of Jesus to entail a social and political ministry. The care of the needy and poor was a central concern in early Christianity. Later when society took over some responsibility for the poor and needy, the church turned its attention to concern with how the state met the requirements of social justice. For example, in the fourth century the church criticized the tax policies of Constantine's empire because they favored the rich at the expense of small farmers. In medieval times church leaders and theologians often praised or criticized political leaders on matters of social justice such as the need for legislation to provide for the poor, the sick, and abandoned children. During all these periods, the church's obligation to speak out on social and political issues has stemmed not from a greater expertise in the political and economic realm, but from its obligation to bring the values of Jesus to bear on the historical situation.

Liberation theologians throughout the globe have shown us that in today's complex societies there are many sinful systems and structures. The role of the church is therefore to call for change in those systems. In the United States this has involved criticism and advocacy, and even civil disobedience in relation to policies on nuclear weapons or the apartheid policy of South Africa. In Latin America attempts to change structures have often meant martyrdom in solidarity with the poor and oppressed. Many Christians in both countries see such actions as crucial if the church is to fulfill its mission of helping to bring about the reign of justice and love which is the heart of Jesus' message, and for which he gave his life.

SUMMARY

The church did not come into being through any one action of Jesus, but evolved gradually as the Spirit enabled the early disciples to be faithful to his vision and mission. Christian faith continues to require a community to support and nourish it. Although institutional aspects of the church give rise to negative experiences and raise questions for many Christians, it is not possible to sustain Christian life without institutional forms. However, the church is ever in need of reform and renewal if it is to remain faithful to Jesus' vision and spirit. We also need more modest images of the church, such as a community of disciples, which remind us that the church is not yet the reign of God but that it does have a mandate to help realize Jesus' vision of justice and love.

Questions and Exercises

1. How would you answer the question, Why the church?

2. Did Jesus found the church? If so, how?

3. If you belong to a Christian community, indicate the ways in which that community has been important for your faith. If you do not belong to such a community, indicate any areas where you have felt the need for such support.

4. What positive aspects are there to the church as institution? What do you find most difficult to accept in the church's institutional life?

5. Agree or disagree with this statement and give reasons to support your position: Whenever beliefs are held by more than one person and sustained over time, they become institutionalized.

6. What images best express your idea of what the church is or should be?

7. Explain what it means to call the church a community of disciples. What is your response to this description of the church?

8. How would you describe the church's relationship to the political sphere?

Suggestions for Further Reading

Robert McAfee Brown, *Liberation Theology: An Introductory Guide* (Westminster, 1993). Explores the new mode of thinking about the church found in liberation theology, and focuses on its meaning for North Americans.

James H. Cone. *For My People: Black Theology and the Black Church* (Orbis, 1984). Historical and theological perspectives on the black struggle for justice and freedom and the problem of the black/white church dichotomy.

Avery Dulles, *Models of the Church*. Expanded edition (Image Books, 1987). Describes and compares the different models that together make up a balanced theology of the church.

Heinrich Fries and Karl Rahner, *Unity of the Churches: An Actual Possibility* (Paulist, 1985). Deals with the issues in the current ecumenical dialogue among the churches, proposing a resolution.

Michael J. Himes and Kenneth R. Himes, *Fullness of Faith: The Public Significance of Theology* (Paulist, 1993). Grounds the church's social teaching in theology, and shows how the political stance of Christians is one with their faith.

Virginia Hoffman, *Birthing a Living Church* (Crossroad, 1988). Presents a vision of a new church structure coming to birth in the experience of small, intentional communities of faith.

Ada María Isasi-Díaz and Yolanda Tarango, *Hispanic Women: Prophetic Voice in the Church* (Harper & Row, 1988). Shows how the experience of Hispanic women is calling the church to become a community of people in which women play a central role.

Letty Russell, *Church in the Round: Feminist Interpretation of the Church* (Westminster, 1993). Reimages the church using the central symbol of a round table where leadership is shared and diversity is welcomed.

CHAPTER 10

Christian Spirituality, Prayer, and Sacraments

The term "spirituality" has grown in popularity in recent decades, and has been employed in many different senses. Basic to most meanings of it, however, is a focus on our lived relationship to the transcendent, or whatever we designate as the source of ultimate meaning in life. It embraces how we experience the transcendent, how we know ourselves in relation to it, and how we live out this relationship.

Spirituality describes our religious experience and the way in which we translate our beliefs into a whole way of life. The spiritual is not the immaterial as contrasted with the bodily or material; it is not one compartment of life, but the deepest dimension of all of life. It is the ultimate ground of our questions, hopes, fears, and loves. Since spirituality concerns our entire personhood in all of our relationships, it often draws on insights from other disciplines, e.g., psychology, sociology, or history. Some contemporary approaches to spirituality, for example, incorporate the thinking of the Swiss psychologist, Carl Jung.

Since there are many beliefs about the divine/human relationship, there are many spiritualities. One way to distinguish them is by descriptive adjectives which identify the belief systems and symbols from which they derive or the persons by and for whom they are developed. Thus we speak of Christian, Jewish, or Buddhist spirituality, and also of Hispanic spirituality and of women's or men's spiritualities. Within Christian spirituality, paths to the holy have been named after the individuals who first taught them, e.g., Ignatian spirituality after the sixteenth-century founder of the Jesuits, St. Ignatius Loyola. Christian spirituality, already rich and diverse in itself, also draws from other spiritualities, influenced, for example, by Native American peoples' profound awareness of divine presence and their concern for all creation.

The widespread interest in spirituality today reveals a hunger in people for contact with the deepest source of energy and creativity. Many fear that our civilization has lost its soul. It is not enough simply to know about the divine; they long to *experience* the holy, and are attracted to paths that show them how to care for the soul. For example, New Age spirituality incorporates beliefs and practices from many religious and philosophical sources and puts them at the service of spiritual development—planetary healing, self-improvement, holistic health, reincarnation, crystals, astrology. Other approaches to soul care focus primarily on finding God in home and family, in art and beauty, in relationships with others.

Adding the adjective *Christian* to the term spirituality means that the life and message of Jesus are decisive in shaping our experience of the sacred. We see ourselves as called to be Christian disciples. We want to become persons whose whole being and life are under the influence of the Spirit of God revealed in Jesus, and we rely on the gifts of his Spirit to bring us to holiness. We also draw on the rich traditions of spiritual life developed through the two thousand years of Christian experience. Everything in this book has to do in one way or another with Christian spirituality. In the remainder of this chapter we focus specifically on prayer and sacraments as two important sources and expressions of Christian spirituality.

CHRISTIAN PRAYER

From the very earliest centuries, prayer has been an important part of Christian life. In exploring Christian prayer we will consider four questions frequently asked about it: 1) Why pray? 2) What is prayer? 3) How should we pray? and 4) Can we judge the quality of our prayer?

Why Pray?

For some people, prayer is almost exclusively an expression of the need for help. They forget about God until they find themselves wanting something badly or caught in a situation they cannot handle alone. Then they cry "Help!"

Many today are looking for a fuller life of prayer. Occasional desperate cries for help are not enough to satisfy their longing for vital contact with the source of life. This search for a deeper relationship with God is movingly disclosed in the diaries of a young Jewish woman who died at Auschwitz in November, 1943, at the age of twenty-nine. Etty Hillesum composed these diaries during the last two years of her life, but they have only recently been discovered and published as *An Interrupted Life*. Her daily reflections reveal not only her intellectual passions and growing understanding of her sexuality, but an independent and vibrant young woman's journey to new spiritual depths. At the heart of this journey is her hunger for prayer. In one of her diary entries she says that there is a really deep well inside her, and in it God dwells. Sometimes she is there too. But often stones and grit block the well and God is buried beneath. Gradually, however, Etty turns more and more naturally to God in prayer—to share her anguish, give praise for the world's beauty, or rest in a presence that sustains her. Her prayer gives her courage and centers her being.

Such a relationship with God is central to Christian existence, as is evident from Jesus' own prayer life as well as the prayer forms that have developed in the Christian tradition. Jesus does teach and urge prayer of petition. He encourages his disciples to ask God for what they need: "Ask and you shall receive, seek and you shall find, knock and it shall be opened to you" (Lk 11:9). He trusts in God, and insists that God gives good gifts to those who ask, so we should be unafraid to ask (Mt 6:11). Our desires are to be broad enough to include petitions for the hoped-for final age. Almost every phrase of the Lord's Prayer refers to this age of God's reign.

However, Jesus' teaching on prayer is not confined to asking God for things. The passion of Jesus' life is his search for God's will in everything. His life and work are sustained by a deep relationship with God, and he believes that communing with God in silence is of great importance. The gospels frequently write of him: "He stayed in a desert place," or "Rising early the next morning, he went off to a lonely place in the desert; there he was absorbed in prayer" (Mk 1:45; 1:35). While Jesus prays to God whenever he can, these attempts to be alone are frequently interrupted by the demands of the crowds that follow him. A closer look at the meaning of prayer will help us understand how solitary prayer and the service of others can be united in our lives as they were in his.

What Is Prayer?

Christian prayer can be described as listening and responding to God's word. But this gives rise to the question,

When and how does God speak? In answering this question, it is helpful to recall what was said in earlier chapters about the ways we encounter God in life. God speaks in nature, in the beauty and majesty of the world around us. God's word also comes to us in history, in the events of our lives. We hear God's word in scripture as well. We can begin our prayer then from our experiences of wonder at a beautiful sunset or majestic mountain peak. We might start with a passage of scripture. Or we can begin with the restlessness and loneliness of our hearts, our experiences of power and achievement, a painful conversation, or a recent gift of love. Jesus' prayer was such a response to the events of his life. The gospels show Jesus turning to prayer when he struggles to understand his vocation, when he chooses his twelve apostles, when he is facing death.

Prayer is expressive of all our experiences: sorrow, gratitude, fear, forgiveness, trust, grief, inadequacy. When people are genuinely themselves in prayer, these emotions arise honestly and spontaneously. That is why the analogy of friendship is frequently used for Christian prayer. We can afford to be ourselves with our friends, and bring to the relationship whatever is paramount for us at a given time. Sometimes we listen attentively to a friend; at other times we speak. Gradually the relationship transforms us. So it is with prayer. Jesus teaches us to understand prayer as a relationship with an intimate and loving friend, a relationship that sustains and heals our lives.

How Should We Pray?

The essence of Christian prayer is a relationship with God which enables us to support God's purpose in the world. Since prayer is a relationship, it takes a variety of forms in individual lives, and these forms are less important than the relationship which they nourish. People pray while walking, dancing, singing, reading scripture, or writing in a journal. They pray alone as well as with their families or communities. Prayer can be a formal activity, with special times set aside in the day. Or prayer can be an habitual attitude, an awareness that makes it natural to walk through the challenges and blessings of the day with God.

The French philosopher and political activist, Simone Weil, saw prayer as "waiting for God," as attentive listening. Teilhard de Chardin, the Jesuit scientist and religious thinker, described prayer both as a descent within himself to the center of his creativity, and as union with all of creation. St. Augustine found God in the recollection of the events of his life, for he believed that God spoke through such memories. Thomas Merton reminds us that prayer is a gift, and we should let the prayer pray itself within us. Just as an apple ripens by opening itself to the sun, so we should let the gifts of God move through us. Some Christians today are learning from eastern prayer forms and are incorporating the body more fully into prayer through yoga or Zen meditation. There are many paths of prayer, and each individual will pray as no one else prays, since our prayer expresses the uniqueness of our relationship with God. There is no one way to pray.

Can We Judge the Quality of Our Prayer?

One question many people ask is, "How do I know if my prayer is any good?" When people request something from God and do not receive it, they sometimes think their prayer was not heard. Huckleberry Finn is reported to have prayed for a fishing pole and hooks. When he got only the pole, he gave up on prayer. Such reactions miss the fact that God's purposes and vision are much larger than ours. While the gospels encourage us to make our needs known, they also tell us that we must be open, as Jesus was, to having our understanding of God's purpose enlarged and transformed.

All teaching on Christian prayer emphasizes the fact that we cannot judge the quality of our prayer by the feelings we experience during it. Warm feelings do not necessarily mean good prayer. A lack of feeling does not necessarily mean fruitless prayer. The criterion of Christian prayer is not feelings but the pattern of life it produces. We judge our prayer by the kind of life it enables us to live. If our relationship to the God of Jesus is growing stronger through prayer, the results will be greater peace with God, ourselves, and others; an open, compassionate attitude; focus on God's concerns; and a growing freedom to be our true selves without fear.

CHRISTIAN SACRAMENTS

Since the Protestant reformation in the sixteenth century, Christians have differed about what role to give sacraments in their lives. In part because of the abuses they saw in the church's use of the sacraments, some Protestant reformers put less emphasis on them, or eliminated certain sacraments completely. Today Roman Catholics celebrate seven sacraments: baptism, confirmation, eucharist, reconciliation, anointing, holy orders, and matrimony. Most Protestant churches recognize just two of these sacraments, baptism and eucharist.

In this section we will reflect first on why there are sacraments at all. Then we will explore the meaning of the two sacraments which all the churches recognize, and finally consider briefly the meaning of the other five Roman Catholic sacraments.

Why Are There Sacraments?

In a broad sense, a sacrament is any visible, material reality—water, fire, a human person, a human action—which reveals and makes present the saving love of God. According to this description, all of life can be sacramental, since all creation is suffused with the sacred. More narrowly defined, the term sacrament refers to the church's liturgical rituals such as baptism and eucharist. In what follows, our main focus is on the sacramental rituals, but we want to show how these rituals open us to the sacramentality of all of life.

We can understand the significance of the sacraments only if we know how important rituals are in human life generally. Ritual is a primary form of human expression. Since we are embodied spirits, even the deepest spiritual realities in our lives need to be spoken in a bodily way. When we want to say "I love you" to someone, the first thing we are aware of is that words are inadequate. So we say it through a kiss, an embrace, a rose, a poem. These are all symbols, ways of embodying our spirit, giving expression to our deepest thoughts and feelings. Rituals are actions which incorporate such symbols. One young woman, who had experienced a difficult relationship with her father through the years, found that at the time of his death she needed a ritual to express the reconciliation that had taken place in the last hours of his life. Her father had always loved the ocean, and had passed on this love of ocean beaches to his children. The afternoon after his death she walked along the water's edge, remembering special times and praying for forgiveness. He had not been a perfect father; she had not been a perfect daughter. While praying for a healing of memories, she found a small cockle shell with the colors of the sunset. She kept it in her pocket all day, and that night at the funeral home, she slipped it into her father's pocket. This simple ritual captures the human need for symbolic action, for a way to express realities that are too deep for words.

Ritual gives meaning to life. Roman Catholic theologian Bernard Cooke explains how sacraments transform the meaning of human experience. Our experience of any reality depends on the meaning it has for us. An examination can, for example, be either a terrible ordeal or a challenging part of learning, depending on the meaning assigned to it. When our possessions are stolen from us, our deepest grief is over the ones with "sentimental value," i.e., those associated with certain precious persons and situations. They can never be replaced, even if we have insurance, because they are much more to us than what they are worth monetarily. It was their *meaning* that really counted. We have countless experiences in life: we live certain careers, raise families, grow old. But what do these experiences mean? Many do not see any meaning in what they do or experience. And death, which overshadows and ends every life, is the most meaningless experience of all.

Through his life, death, and resurrection, Jesus invests all of human life with fresh meaning, changing the significance of its most basic realities: friendship, meals, sickness, birth, death. Jesus proclaims that God is present in all of ordinary life. God is in the joys and sorrows, the hopes and disappointments, of daily life. The sacraments are intense experiences of this sacramentality of all of life; they awaken us to this reality of God's presence and keep it alive in us. Baptism focuses the grace found in *every* acceptance into human community, as well as the mysterious sacredness of all water. Marriage highlights the presence and love of God within *every* human friendship, as well as the mysterious sacredness of human sexuality. The eucharist draws out the deepest meaning of *every* meal in which human beings share what they have and seek peace and union with one another, as well as the wonderful goodness of food and drink. The official sacraments of a Christian community, whatever their number, make clear that all of creation is sacred. They open our eyes to the fact that grace is everywhere.

In *Pilgrim at Tinker Creek*, the Pulitzer Prize-winning writer, Annie Dillard, speaks of the importance of such ability to see. She says that when she was growing up in Pittsburgh, and was six or seven years old, she had a compulsion to hide a penny, a precious penny of her own, where someone would find it. She hid it along some stretch of highway or up a street. Sometimes she would cradle it in the roots of a sycamore tree or in the hole left by a chipped-off piece of sidewalk. If people ignored it, she would draw an arrow and make a sign with chalk that said, "Surprise ahead." She wanted to offer people a free gift from the universe. Her point is that the world is filled with unwrapped gifts and free surprises for those who know how to see. The world is filled with grace. But who stops to pick it up? Do we really take time to see? The purpose of the sacraments is to nourish this sense of the sacredness of even the smallest details of human life.

Christian Baptism

As soon as groups arose out of faith in the resurrection of Jesus, they needed to introduce new members into their communities. The common means of initiation was the sacrament of baptism. Scripture attests to the universal practice of baptism in the early church.

The early Christians use a variety of images to describe the new life that comes through baptism. Baptism enables us to participate in Christ's death and resurrection (Rom 6:3-5); it washes away sin (1 Cor 6:11); it is a new birth and an enlightenment by Christ (Jn 3:5; Jn 9; Eph 5:14); it brings a renewal by the Spirit and a liberation into a new humanity in which the divisions of sex, race, and social status are overcome (Tit 3:5; Gal 3:27-28).

The central symbol of baptism is water. Reflecting on water's rich meaning helps us to grasp the significance of baptism. Just as Israel passed through the Sea of Reeds to salvation and freedom, so Christians who move through the waters of baptism are immersed in the liberating death of Jesus where the power of sin is broken. They know a new freedom in the power of the resurrection.

Sometimes Christians wonder if anything really happens to them in baptism. Many are baptized as infants and have no recollection of the event. Baptism is not meant to be a sort of magical event that makes us Christians in an instant. It is an initiation into a community which supports the life-long process of becoming a disciple of Jesus Christ. The ritual of baptism must be seen as gateway to this larger reality, initiation into the mystery of Christ by initiation into the Christian community. Those who are baptized as infants are to be guided by the community over time into a personal understanding and acceptance of the meaning of their baptism. The same is true even of adult baptism.

Christian Eucharist

As he faced the certain reality of his approaching death, Jesus asked his disciples to continue their custom of community meals in memory of him. At a final meal

> ...he took some bread, and when he had given thanks, broke it and gave it to them, saying, "This is my body which will be given for you; do this as a memorial of me." He did the same with the cup after supper, and said, "This cup is the new covenant in my blood which will be poured out for you" (Lk 22:19-22).

Even though Jesus would no longer be visible to them, he would be present as they came together to break the bread and share the cup, remembering him and sharing their lives with one another. Luke's story of the disciples on the road to Emmaus is about this same experience:

> Now while he was with them at table, he took the bread and said the blessing; then he broke it and handed it to them. And their eyes were opened and they recognized him; but he had vanished from their sight (24:30-32).

All through the centuries, Jesus' followers have gathered together to eat bread and drink wine, convinced that their Lord is present with them in this ritual action. The meal is also a way of giving thanks for the gift of communion and friendship with one another and with the God revealed in Jesus. Moreover, it is a time for Christians to reaffirm their commitment to Jesus' vision of God's reign. This ritual celebration is the central action of Christian worship.

The first eucharist was set within another ancient ritual, the Jewish Passover meal. During this meal the Jews reenact and so make present again the saving action of God in bringing them from bondage in Egypt to freedom, the exodus. This meal continues to be for Christians a freedom supper, but now what it commemorates is God's saving action in the life, death, and resurrection of Jesus. The eucharist is meant to be above all a shared meal of love and friendship among all those united with Jesus and committed to his cause. Eating a meal with someone is a sign of intimacy. When the Christians of Corinth fall to quarreling with one another and allow divisions and hierarchies to prevail in their "community," Paul has to step in and point out the contradiction in their shared eucharist (1 Cor 11:18-21). It is a broken, meaningless symbol.

The eucharist is the center of Christian life, then,

because it expresses in ritual all the central beliefs of Christians. It is about sharing, about love and mutual respect and service to others, about forgiveness and salvation, about thanksgiving to God for all God's gifts, about Jesus' presence in the midst of life and Christians' commitment to bringing about God's reign. This meal is repeated again and again because it makes present these mysteries with power in the lives of Christians.

Christian sacraments are at once gifts of God and human creations. Through symbolic actions, we experience the message of Jesus' life, death, and resurrection: the divine presence in all of human life gradually transforming it into the reign of God.

The Other Five Roman Catholic Sacraments

Roman Catholicism recognizes five additional sacraments: reconciliation, confirmation, matrimony, holy orders, and the anointing of the sick. Latin American theologian Juan Luis Segundo offers us a key to understanding the essence of all of them, as well as of baptism and eucharist. Each of them brings the paschal mystery (Jesus' death/ resurrection) to bear on a critical situation in human life. In baptism, it is initiation into life-giving community. The issue is: to belong or not to belong, a critical matter for anyone, since we all depend vitally on belonging if we are to be secure and on community if we are to grow and develop. Baptism brings the death/resurrection of Jesus to bear as saving mystery on that critical situation. It is God's own welcome to us, and it shows us what true community should be.

As life goes on, even though Christians hold such a vision of community, they sometimes fall out with and injure one another. The sacrament of reconciliation brings the death/resurrection of Jesus to that critical situation, with its message of forgiveness and its proclamation of God's gift of new beginnings.

Puberty is a critical passage in life, in which we move from childhood to adulthood with all its responsibilities. The questions are, what kind of person will we make of ourselves, and what directions will we take in life? Confirmation, usually celebrated today at this juncture, brings the paschal mystery to these important questions, illumining this passage with Jesus' supporting presence and example. Marriage marks another passage, from the single life to partnership with another. It is fraught with peril, as the high divorce rate shows. The sacrament of matrimony brings Jesus' death/ resurrection to this situation too, teaching the couple that they too will have to die and rise many times in keeping their love commitment to one another, and offering them Jesus' support.

Holy orders sets aside certain individuals to serve the community in developing their life of faith. It is a charge heavy with responsibility. This sacrament takes the ordained person into the death/resurrection mystery of Jesus as light and strength for a ministry to be lived after his own example. The frailties of age or serious illness bring us face to face with the final passage, the awesome mystery of our own mortality. The sacrament of anointing brings Jesus' own dying and rising to our assistance, consoling us with the hope of healing and resurrection. All of these situations are quite specific. How does the eucharist fit into this picture? It is the maintenance sacrament of the Christian community, keeping the paschal mystery in the forefront of our minds as we meet the challenges and choices of daily living.

In Roman Catholic theology, each of the sacraments is a personal encounter with Christ. What Segundo brings to clearer focus is that each of them addresses some critical passage in life when the forces of death threaten particularly, and each brings not only Jesus himself but specifically the saving mystery of his death/resurrection to that situation.

Sacraments are not peculiar to Christianity. All religions have rituals. This is because humans are both body and spirit, and cannot hear and respond to the deepest realities of life unless they perform them in ritual actions enriched by symbols such as water and words, rings and oil, bread and wine.

SUMMARY

Christian spirituality is the concrete way Christians live out their relationship with the God of Jesus. Prayer and sacraments have been two of the crucial sources and expressions of that spirituality from earliest times. Christian prayer, like that of Jesus, nourishes the relationship with God. Jesus taught us to present our needs to God, but prayer should not end there. In prayer we listen to God speaking in nature, history, scripture, and the events of our lives, and respond to this word in a wide variety of ways.

Through symbolic actions such as eating and drinking, baptizing with water, and anointing with oil, Christians continue to open themselves to Jesus' healing presence and power and the new meaning he gives key human experiences. Sacramental celebrations are meant to lead Christians to greater awareness of the sacramentality of all experience.

Questions and Exercises

1. Explain the meaning of spirituality. How is Christian spirituality different from other spiritualities?

2. Describe the key elements in your own spirituality.

3. How would you answer the question, What is prayer? Do you consider prayer to be an essential part of Christian life? Why or why not?

4. List the starting points for prayer mentioned in this chapter. Do any of them appeal to you? If not, what suggestions do you have for approaching prayer?

5. Recall some rituals you have experienced in areas of life other than the religious, e.g., sports, friendships, family celebrations. Describe the symbols and actions that were a part of these rituals and the impact they had on the participants, including yourself.

6. Show what Christian sacraments have to do with a) human expression, b) human meaning, c) the sacred in human life, and d) the paschal mystery.

7. Summarize the meaning of Christian baptism.

8. Explain the meaning of Christian eucharist and then relate that meaning to actual eucharists you have experienced. Where do you find points of convergence and difference?

Suggestions for Further Reading

Wilkie Au, *By Way of the Heart: Toward a Holistic Christian Spirituality* (Paulist, 1989). Shows how to live out Christian habits of the heart and offers guidance for a variety of approaches to prayer.

Leonardo Boff, *Sacraments of Life, Life of the Sacraments* (Pastoral Press, 1987). Original reflections on the sacramentality of daily life that bring its meaning into the realm of experience.

Anthony de Mello, *Sadhana: A Way to God* (Doubleday, 1984). A wide variety of Christian prayer exercises, sometimes incorporating eastern forms, accompanied by reflections on the meaning of prayer.

Michael Downey, ed., *The New Dictionary of Catholic Spirituality* (Liturgical Press, 1993). A variety of authors treat aspects of spirituality in light of church renewal since the Second Vatican Council, with attention to ecumenical and interreligious issues.

Elizabeth A. Dreyer, *Earth Crammed With Heaven: A Spirituality of Everyday Life* (Paulist, 1994). Practical overview of a spirituality for lay Christians that describes everyday life as a sacred space where God and people meet.

Tad Guzie, *The Book of Sacramental Basics* (Paulist, 1982). A readable explanation that describes the sacraments in the context of people's lives.

Joseph Martos, *Doors to the Sacred: An Historical Introduction to the Sacraments in the Catholic Church*. Expanded edition (Triumph Books, 1991). The history and theology of sacramentality and of the seven Roman Catholic sacraments specifically.

World Council of Churches, *Baptism, Eucharist, and Ministry* (World Council of Churches, 1982). The results of fifty years of ecumenical dialogues on the meaning of baptism, eucharist, and ministry.

CHAPTER 11

Care for Creation

A new awareness exists in the global community today, a recognition that numerous ecological perils threaten all living beings on earth. The extinction of species, the pollution of land, air and water, the rapid destruction of forests and massive erosion of soil, the thinning of the ozone layer and global warming—all these developments raise widespread concern. More recently, the link between ecology (the science that studies the relationships among all life forms) and justice has become clear. Excessive consumption and growth-oriented economic practices have not only changed some of the most precious features of our planet; they have led to poverty and loss of hope among human beings.

Christians cannot ignore so crucial a contemporary issue. Our faith is meant to illumine and guide us in each cultural context. What does it have to say to this pressing problem? Can it speak to those who have lost hope in the possibility of our planet's future survival? How, in turn, might an ecological worldview—a vision that sees all life forms existing in communion—enrich our faith?

We do not look to Christian faith for a detailed program of action regarding environmental problems, but rather for insight into the place of nature in God's plan. Christians might be able to contribute something substantive to the development of what has been called "ecological conscious-ness," a heightened awareness of how we view and interact with the environment. With this goal in mind, Christian theologians have responded in several ways: 1) by providing a critique of those aspects of the western Christian tradition which have helped produce the crisis; 2) by showing that scripture and tradition offer a rich basis for ecological ethics and action; and 3) by developing a spirituality shaped by concern for ecology. We will explore each of these contributions.

INTERPRETING THE BIBLE ON CREATION

How we understand what the bible says about the relationship of human beings to the rest of nature is crucial. Critics argue that Judaism and Christianity have supported a view of human dominion that demeans the rest of nature. Even the Christian understanding of the incarnation, they contend, gives humanity the central place in the plan of creation and redemption, reducing the rest of creation to secondary status.

It is true that certain biblical passages have been inter-preted to mean that the earth is raw material for humans to use as they wish. The biblical injunction to subdue the earth, found in the first of the creation accounts, seems to support an imperialistic stance toward the material world. After recounting the making of woman and man, the account says:

> God blessed them, saying, "Be fruitful and multiply, fill the earth and conquer it. Be masters of the sea, the birds of heaven and all living animals on the earth" (Gen 1:28).

This passage has usually been interpreted to support an attitude reducing the nonhuman to mere means to human ends. Influenced by this idea, we speak of mastering the land, dominating nature, conquering space.

Going along with the language of dominion is a hierarchical reading of the creation story. Creation is conceived in the image of a ladder or pyramid. God is at the top, and beneath God are men. Next in the hierarchy are women and children, and beneath them are animals and plants, then the inanimate parts of creation. Just as God rules over man, so man is to rule over woman. In *Green Paradise Lost*, Elizabeth Dobson Gray shows how the same thinking that justifies the subordination of women blesses humanity's subjugation of nature.

There have been several attempts to reinterpret what Genesis says about subduing the earth. These call attention to other themes in Genesis which caution against a narrow focus on human dominion. One is emphasis on the limitations of human power; the dominion envisioned is stewardship over an earth that ultimately belongs to God: "To you (God) belong the earth and all that it holds, the world and all who live in it" (Ps 24:1). Human beings are caretakers of creation because they are made in the image of God (Gen 2:27), and therefore are to mirror God's own way of acting, being good stewards or responsible caretakers of the earth.

Interpretations of human dominion must also take account of the importance the bible accords every aspect of creation. Humans do have unique value, but other species on the planet also have intrinsic worth. Each makes a distinctive contribution to the whole. The psalmist proclaims:

> God, what variety you have created,
> arranging everything so wisely!
> Earth is completely full of things you have made:
> among them the vast expanse of ocean,

> teeming with countless creatures,
> creatures large and small (Ps 104:24-25).

The psalms frequently dwell in praise and thanksgiving on the details of creation: dark, misty rain clouds; thornbushes and thistles; grass on the mountainside; snow, frost and hail. God takes pleasure in all of creation, and creation responds with joy and praise.

> You crown the year with your bounty,
> abundance flows wherever you pass;
> the desert pastures overflow,
> the hillsides are wrapped in joy,
> the meadows are dressed in flocks,
> the valleys are clothed in wheat,
> what shouts of joy, what singing (Ps 65:11-13)!

Many of the psalms celebrate the integrity of the earth, the fact that the whole creation is good and every part of it counts. The poets of the bible remind us also of the interrelationship among all aspects of nature.

The fourteenth-century hermitess, Julian of Norwich, provides another image for this sense of the whole. Julian's teachings center on an appreciation of the goodness of God's world. She uses imagery which weaves elements of nature—spring rain, seaweed swept by the movement of waves—with reflections on the divine. In one of her most familiar passages, she says that God showed her a little object, the size of a hazelnut. She held it in the palm of her hand, and it was round as a ball. She puzzled, wondering what it might be. The answer came: "It is all that is made."

Creation's importance, then, does not lie simply in its support of human life. Genesis describes God as pronouncing the creation good before human life was ever created: "God saw that it was good" (Gen 1:21, 25).

God's Covenant with All of Creation

In the bible, God makes a covenant or sacred agreement not only with humans, but with all of creation. This is clear in Genesis chapters 8 and 9, which tell the story of Noah and the flood. The agreement with Noah and his descendants is described as a covenant between God and the rest of the earth.

> God said, "Here is the sign of the covenant I make between myself and you and every living creature with you for all generations: I set my bow in the clouds and it shall be a sign of the covenant between me and the earth. When I gather the clouds over the earth and the bow appears in the clouds, I will recall the covenant between myself and you and every living creature of every kind" (Gen 9:12-15).

In this vision, humanity is presented not as over and above nature, but as a part of it.

In the new world order symbolized by the promise of the rainbow the unity of all of creation will be restored. The prophet Hosea makes this clear.

> Then I will make a covenant on behalf of Israel with the wild beasts, the birds of the air, and things that creep on the earth, and I will break bow and sword and weapon of war and sweep them off the earth, so that all living creatures may lie down without fear (Hos 2:20).

The prophet's pleas for justice include the restoration of humanity's broken relationship with creation. The covenant calls for a situation in which all creatures live together in mutual respect and companionship. The fracturing of these relationships is evidence of the presence of sin in the world.

Moving from the Hebrew scriptures to the New

Testament description of the covenant, we find similar testimony to the importance of the earth. In the biblical view, creation and redemption are different aspects of one reality. The redemption accomplished in Christ is not limited to the individual person, but extends to the whole creation. Just as sin destroys the harmonious relationship between God, humanity, and creation, so Christ's reconciliation restores the total harmony. A holistic understanding of redemption is expressed, for example, by Paul.

> ...but creation still retains the hope of being freed, like us, from its slavery to decadence, to enjoy the same freedom and glory as the children of God. From the beginning till now the entire creation, as we know, has been groaning in one great act of giving birth; and not only creation, but all of us who possess the first-fruits of the Spirit, we too groan inwardly as we wait for our bodies to be set free (Rom 8:21-23).

Reconciliation in the biblical sense puts every creature in community with every other. We are put right in our relationship to the material world. Nature is now no longer an object, but a companion. Sharing in Christ's work of redemption calls us to work not just for the salvation of humanity but for the restoration of all the earth.

The covenantal relationship between humans and all other forms of life, the fact that we are united as one family by one source of life, calls us to treat all creatures with awareness both of their otherness and of their kinship with us. All beings have their own purpose, their own right to exist, their own relationship to God and to other beings. This leads us to encounter all of nature as "Thou" rather than "It," as fellow beings with their own integrity. The Jewish philosopher, Martin Buber, developed this insight in his understanding of I-Thou relationships as the primary encounter with God, in and through not only other human beings but trees and other living beings.

The Divine Presence in Nature

We saw in the last chapter that the term sacrament refers not only to the official church sacraments, but to anything that has the capacity to reveal the divine. In this sense the entire universe is sacramental. A sacramental approach to ecology holds that the entire cosmos bodies forth God to us. Its sacramental transparency gives the natural world an intrinsic value that should lead us to concern for its preservation and provide the basis for responsible planning. How can we wreak destruction on creatures we know to be incarnations of God's beauty, goodness, and love?

Thomas Berry, a Passionist priest, is one of the proponents of this sacramental approach. Along with Matthew Fox he represents a movement sometimes called "creation spirituality," an effort to address centuries of narrow focus on human beings while ignoring the rest of God's creation. For Berry, the universe is the primary revelation of God. Berry claims that most people today do not have a story of the cosmos which helps them understand on a daily basis how they and other created beings fit into the total scheme of things. If we have a sense of the divine, he says, it is because we live amid the kind of mystery and splendor found in such things as the shape of an orchid or the coloring of fish in the sea. The sacred character of our habitat demands from us a sense of reverence toward the earth and all its inhabitants. We need a rebirth of wonder at the luminous quality of everyday reality, which will give us a sense of belonging not as lords over creation but as that part of creation which is gifted with self-consciousness and awareness of the whole. This will enable us both to acknowledge our special place in a marvelous universe, and to live in courteous communion with all other creatures.

Others too see the sacramental quality of all creation as the basis for an environmental ethic. In *The Body of God: An Ecological Theology*, Protestant theologian Sallie McFague uses the metaphor of earth as the body of God in order to speak of it as sacrament of the divine. We are invited to see ourselves as living in the body of God, a body in which God's liberating, healing, and inclusive love reigns, particularly on behalf of the oppressed. We are invited to see the creator in the creation, the source of all existence in and through all that is bodied forth.

McFague wants to bring the Christian faith into dialogue with the picture of reality presented to us by contemporary science. From this "creation account" we learn that we are radically interrelated and interdependent with everything else in the universe, particularly on our own planet. We exist in a vast community of individuals within an ecosystem, and need to live in ways that honor the interdependencies. When we speak of ourselves as guardians or caretakers of our planet, it must be within this view of our place in the whole.

Nature as Filled with Future Promise

One criticism of the sacramental approach is that it does not take seriously enough the awful oppression that is part of the mystery and splendor of the universe. Nature not only evokes admiration; it also presents a saga of struggle, brutality, loss, and death. The bible's eschatological perspective is therefore important as a companion to the sacramental. Eschatology (from the Greek *eschatos*, "the furthest, the last") has to do with the last things: the end of the world, heaven and hell. It also includes our hope for the ultimate fulfillment of God's covenant promises. We will be treating eschatology more fully in the next chapter, but here we want to note its significance for ecology. Through it we come to see nature too as awaiting its fulfillment.

In *The Promise of Nature*, Roman Catholic theologian John Haught treats this aspect of the biblical message. He shows that the theme of promise for the future and God's fidelity to this promise is central to both the Hebrew and Christian scriptures. If, at first glance, eschatology might seem to call our attention and energies away from involvement in healing this world's ecological ills, more fundamentally it underscores our anticipation in faith of God's regeneration of *the entire creation*. Eschatology then does not lead to escape from this world, but points us toward its fulfillment. Nature is not something from which we separate ourselves in order to find a final human fulfillment, but a reality to which we are forever related and whose resurrection to new life we expect to occur along with our own. In other words, the earth is our lasting habitat, not just a place we are passing through on our way to another truer home.

An important part of Christian tradition sees Christ as the *cosmic* manifestation of God, as both creator and redeemer of the cosmos, not just of human beings. This vision of the role of Christ in the beginning and end of "*all things*" is found in Paul, John, and Hebrews. One of its fullest expressions is in Colossians:

> He is the image of the invisible God, the firstborn of all creation; for in him all things in heaven and on earth were created, things visible and invisible, whether thrones or dominions or rulers or powers—all things have been created through him and for him....For in him all the fullness of God was pleased to dwell and through him God was pleased to reconcile to himself all things, whether on earth or in heaven, by making peace through the blood of his cross (Col 1:15-20).

A contemporary version of this cosmological theology is the creation-centered spirituality propounded by Matthew Fox. In his *The Coming of the Cosmic Christ* Fox presents Christ as the immanent Wisdom of God present in the whole cosmos as its principle of interconnected and abundant life. The cosmic Christ is not only the foundation of the original blessing in all creation, but also the direction of creation's fulfillment. The cosmic Christ is therefore another name for both the original and the final blessing.

While they have contributed to developing in many people a sense of reverence for the wonders of nature, Fox and other creation spirituality writers are often criticized for an unbounded optimism which fails to address the oppression and evil in nature. An eschatological interpretation of creation is needed, it is felt, to temper our romanticizing of the universe. When we acknowledge that nature's promise is not yet fully realized, we are able to offer it our reverence and work to conserve it while also accommodating its dark side, tolerating its deficiencies and even its ugliness. We ourselves are part of the problem.

When nature is seen as promise as well as present sacrament of the divine, it is all right that it is less than perfect. Because it is not yet fully revelatory of God, it can be both beautiful and bloody. Nature writers are eloquent not only on the grace but also on the violence in creation. It is plain enough that the world is not yet finished.

ELEMENTS OF AN ECOLOGICAL SPIRITUALITY

As we saw in the last chapter, spirituality is the lived experience of faith. Efforts to live out the implications of a Christian ecological theology have given rise to some fresh strands in Christian spirituality as well as a renewed appreciation of traditional elements.

The first is contemplation. Care of the earth must be rooted in prayer, which prepares us for nature's revelations and opens us to the presence of God in the world. We usually call this kind of prayer contemplation. It is a long and loving look at reality, the opening of ourselves to the presence of God's beauty, power, and mystery. When we contemplate a stretch of rolling hills, the clear waters of a mountain lake, or the first blossoms of a tree in springtime, we are not thinking of ways to put these things to work for us, as the technological mind does. We are simply taking them in, standing before them in reverence, appreciating them as manifestations of God. Contemplation is a wholly nonpragmatic approach to reality. It engenders gratitude for the gift of life and passion for the well-being of all things.

The Jesuit scientist and religious thinker, Pierre Teilhard de Chardin, leads into this kind of prayer when he speaks of the world as the outward and visible presence of God. Opening to this presence means learning again how to see the world. Teilhard articulates this vision in "Mass on the World," an essay in his *Hymn of the Universe*. While on a scientific expedition he found himself one day in China's Ordos desert without the chalice or the bread and wine he needed to offer mass. It was the feast of the Transfiguration, and Teilhard's thoughts turned to the divine presence in the entire universe. So he made the whole earth his altar, and lifted up as his offering the whole of creation. Teilhard's spirituality was necessarily cosmic in scope. As a paleontologist, he saw creation from the perspective of time. He knew the cosmos was billions of years old, that human life appeared on the scene only a few million years ago, and that our present conditions of life represent only the last few minutes, relatively speaking, of a very long evolution stretching out into the future.

If Teilhard taught us to see creation from the perspective

of time, contemporary spiritual writer Annie Dillard helps us notice nature's detailed complexity and intricacy. Her approach has been described as praying with one's eyes open. Dillard says she looked up and about, began to see, and was filled with wonder at creation. When we do this, she says, we notice perhaps for the first time the way a wave rises above the ocean horizon, translucent and shot with lights. We listen to the mockingbird and not only puzzle at its song, but ponder the question, "Why is it beautiful?" As we pray in this way, the realization deepens that creation is God's rather than ours. Because it is God's, no one should be deprived of its gifts; nor should anyone hoard them.

Compassion and solidarity flow from a vision of the universe in which connection is a central motif. To be a self in this vision is not to be separate and isolated, but rather to be deeply related to all other beings in the universe. In her novel, *The Temple of My Familiar*, Alice Walker describes this perspective.

> Helped are those who love the Earth, their mother, and willingly suffer that she may not die; in their grief over her pain they will weep rivers of blood, and in their joy in her lively response to love, they will converse with trees....

> Helped are those who find the courage to do at least one small thing each day to help the existence of another— plant, animal, river, human being. They shall be joined by a multitude of the timid.

Compassion is the resultant expression of a worldview in which we understand ourselves and all of nature to be members of the one body Paul describes to the Corinthians. Compassion is the root of justice, another key concern in an ecological spirituality.

Concern for both the environment and the poor calls

for a change of lifestyle by affluent countries, who must consume less and share more. Justice is due the poor and oppressed because, as Jesus taught us, the earth and all that belongs to it are God's. Jesus asked us to show concern for the outcasts of creation, whoever and whatever they might be at any time. It is nature itself in our time that is most oppressed, vulnerable, and in need of some good news.

It is our tendency to isolate God from creation, forgetting the teaching of Jesus, which allows the ecological, technological and nuclear threats to our world to go unchecked. The prophetic challenge of the New Testament is a sweeping vision of reconciliation. If the goods of the earth exist for all, then concern for the poor, reverence for nature, and the protection of the environment all go together.

Christian ecofeminist spirituality is a recent approach whose proponents wish to transform both human oppression and environmental abuse. This spirituality stresses the connection between the male domination of women and the human domination of nature, discerning the same pattern of oppression running through ecological devastation, poverty, and war. For example, deforestation often displaces indigenous people. Hazardous waste sites are usually located near poor neighborhoods or nations. International trade policies hurt both the poor and the earth. In *Gaia and God: An Ecofeminist Theology of Earth Healing*, Rosemary Ruether argues that if we are to heal the broken cosmos, we must reshape patterns of domination not only between human beings and nature, but between men and women, and rich and poor. For these social patterns are the basis of the wasteful exploitation of the biosphere.

It is clear that we will need to practice restraint if other species and other peoples are going to survive on this earth. To do so we must be deeply convinced that God's purpose in creating is that we *all* find a home we can enjoy. Latin American theologian Leonardo Boff points out that the companionship Francis of Assisi felt toward all creation was born of his understanding of poverty. Poverty is the realization that, as creatures, we are all united in finding the fundamental source of our existence in God.

> Be praised, my Lord, for all your creatures!
> In the first place for the blessed Brother Sun....
> Be praised, my Lord, for our sister, Mother Earth,
>   who nourishes and watches us....

Francis was able to enter into a song of praise with brother sun and sister earth because he had learned how to let things be what they are, refusing to dominate or subjugate them. He understood that he was not over things, but *together* with them, like brothers and sisters in the same family.

SUMMARY

In light of widespread concern for the future of our planet, Christians are recognizing the dangers of a theology which stresses human dominion over the rest of creation. Many resources in the Judaeo-Christian tradition contribute to the kind of ecological sensitivity needed in our time. Among these are the emphasis the psalms give to the uniqueness of every element of the universe, the covenant tradition which tells of God's concern for all of creation, a sacramental view which recognizes the way in which all creatures embody the divine presence, and an eschatological vision which keeps alive an appreciation of the future promise of nature while acknowledging its darker aspects. These are some of the themes in the Christian ecological theology emerging today.

An ecological spirituality accompanies these theological insights. It calls us to a kind of contemplation of all creation which gives rise to reverence and gratitude. From this awareness arises both compassion for all creatures and a commitment to justice so that all beings can find a home here on earth. An ecological spirituality thus calls us to live out core values of the gospel.

Questions and Exercises

1. How would you describe the ecological crisis? Do you think it is exaggerated or real? What aspects of it mean the most to you personally?

2. What is meant by the theme of human dominion, and how has it been biblically justified? Recount any ways in which you have seen this belief at work in the human response to nature.

3. Indicate strands in the bible which present a different understanding of the relationship between human beings and the rest of creation. Which of these is most convincing to you? How do the images they suggest—companion, partner, earth-keeper, guardian—contrast with that of dominion?

4. Explain the meaning of a sacramental approach to creation. How can it contribute to ecological sensitivity?

5. Why do we need to keep alive a sense of the future promise of creation? What evidence have you seen of the darker side of nature?

6. Name the key elements of an ecological spirituality as presented in this chapter. From your own experience, would you add any others?

7. Spend some time in quiet contemplation of an aspect of nature—a flower, a blade of grass, an old-growth forest, a rain- or snowstorm. Notice what thoughts and feelings arise in you.

8. Explain the link between ecological concern and justice. Are you drawn to any action in your own life in light of the connection between them?

Suggestions for Further Reading

Thomas Berry, *The Dream of the Earth* (Sierra Club Books, 1988). One of the most influential thinkers on the nature of the cosmos and our place in its future presents his compelling poetic vision.

Charles Cummings, *Eco-Spirituality: Toward a Reverent Life* (Paulist, 1991). Provides a spirituality rooted in reverence for God's creation and the new creation in Christ, and includes practical models and resources for action.

Kathleen Fischer, *Reclaiming the Connections: A Contemporary Spirituality* (Sheed & Ward, 1990). Offers a clear and practical vision of the interconnectedness of all creation, and shows how to mend the divisions which threaten our planet.

Lorna Green, *Earth Age: A New Vision of God, the Human, and the Earth* (Paulist, 1994). Moves from the traditions responsible for the destruction of the earth to a new way of thinking about the universe, spirit, the earth, and ourselves.

John F. Haught, *The Promise of Nature: Ecology and Cosmic Purpose* (Paulist, 1993). A theologian reflects on the ecological crisis as a challenge and an opportunity for the transformation of religion.

Dieter T. Hessel, ed., *After Nature's Revolt: Eco-Justice and Theology* (Augsburg, 1992). Essays on assessing the Christian legacy of dominion over creation, and creating an ethic of eco-justice and a spirituality for the future.

Sallie McFague, *The Body of God: An Ecological Theology* (Fortress Press, 1993). Explores the relationship between the earth crisis and our notion of God, and presents a new model for conceiving God and Christian existence.

Rosemary Radford Ruether, *Gaia and God: An Ecofeminist Theology of Earth Healing* (HarperSanFrancisco, 1992). Examines Christianity's responsibility for the ecological crisis and finds resources within Christian theology for a new beginning.

CHAPTER 12

The End of the World, Heaven, and Hell

Ever since the beginning of Christianity, some people have predicted the imminent return of Christ and the end of the world. Popular eschatology or end-time speculation attracts numerous followers in every era. Basing their calculations on symbolic material from the books of Daniel and Revelation, material such as the thousand-year period or the number 666 associated with the antichrist, these prophets of the end-times have prepared various timetables of the last days. Many of the issues raised about the future transformation of human history are much discussed in our day, particularly as the second millennium draws to a close. Interest in them is not new, however.

In 1812, when Napoleon and his army invaded Moscow, there were groups of Russian believers convinced that the apocalypse had come and Napoleon was the antichrist. During the 1930s popular prophets believed that Benito Mussolini was the antichrist; during World War II, Hitler was nominated. Over the years, different groups have been certain that they knew the exact date of Christ's return. In the 1970s the number-one best-selling book, with the exception of the bible, was Hal Lindsey's *The Late Great Planet Earth*. It has sold more than 15 million copies. In the 1980s the sense of imminent apocalypse even led some to suggest the possibility that God would use nuclear weapons to end human history. Such suggestions make clear the importance of understanding Christian eschatology, or the Christian teaching on the last things.

In this chapter we will reflect on four aspects of the meaning of Christian eschatology: 1) the reign of God already begun; 2) the reign of God in the future; 3) the final judgment, heaven, and hell; and 4) the end of the world and Christian discipleship.

THE REIGN OF GOD ALREADY BEGUN

A central aspect of Jesus' teaching is the message of God's present and coming kingdom. It is difficult for many of us to understand what Jesus meant when he spoke of God's kingdom. Though this term is at the core of his teaching, Jesus never defines it directly. We immediately think of kings and queens and geographical territories. But when Jesus speaks of the kingdom of God, he does not mean a territory. He means the activity of ruling, the reign of God. He is referring to God's cause in the world, whether and how God's presence and power will manifest themselves and be recognized in our lives. God's cause in the world is the great passion of Jesus' life.

The Our Father is a prayer for the coming of God's reign. Jesus prays, and teaches his disciples to pray, that God's name will truly be praised, that God's purpose will be accomplished on earth, that people everywhere will have all they need for life, that all sin will be forgiven and all evil overcome (Lk 11). The kingdom or God's reign is then a way of describing creation's deepest longings for freedom, love, reconciliation and peace. It is what every Christian works for in following Jesus. It is what women and men of good will everywhere yearn and labor for.

God's reign is also the subject of most of Jesus' parables.

It is the great banquet, the royal feast, the ripe harvest, the seed springing up. It is worth giving up everything for, as one would for a rare pearl or a treasure found buried in a field.

Unlike much of the apocalyptic preaching current in his time, Jesus does not emphasize the judgment of a wrathful God on sinners and their exclusion from the reign of God. Although some of his parables contain harsh elements, generally they are stories of compassion and forgiveness. In the parable of the vineyard owner in Matthew 20, the master pays all the workers the same wages, beginning with those who have worked only a single hour. His action violates our sense of fairness; we learn that God does not play exactly by our rules. One of the strongest examples of gratuitous bounty is the parable of the prodigal son in Luke 15, where the father offers extravagant gifts to his wayward son come home. Imaging the world in terms of the bad and the good, sinners and saved, we usually situate ourselves as the good and saved and others as bad and deserving punishment. Only when we recognize ourselves as sinners can we see what good news it is that Jesus' message about the reign of God is based on forgiveness and not the exclusion of the sinner.

Many of the people who came to listen to Jesus were pessimistic about the future. They believed that only a cosmic judgment could destroy the tight hold that evil had on the world. The message of Jesus may have surprised them. Although he sometimes spoke of the coming reign of God, at other times he made clear that it was not a huge cataclysm, but something they could experience now. The reign of God, Jesus says, is among you (Lk 17:20ff). Jesus' presence and healing ministry were themselves unmistakable signs of God's reign in the world. "The darkness is passing away and the true light is already shining" (1 Jn 2:8). Jesus promises that the poor, the hungry, and the downtrodden will come into their own. There will be an end to suffering, pain and death. His life and ministry begin to bring these things about. The new age has begun. Jesus is even now pushing back the powers of evil in the world (Lk 11:20). In the gospel of John the end-time is assumed to be already here. Judgment is passed now, at the hearing of the word (Jn 12:44-48); the passage from death to life takes place now (Jn 11:24-27). Paul reminds us that we are already one with Christ, the risen Lord, through our baptism, already dead and risen in a certain sense (Rom 6:1-11). The end is therefore to be understood not in terms of cosmic disaster, but as the completion of God's work already begun.

As we will see, both the bible and church teaching talk about what is one day going to be—about death, heaven, and hell, about the return of Christ and a new heaven and earth, about the last days and the signs by which the return of Christ can be recognized. But these are also symbolic statements about the Christian present. We can expect for history as a whole what we already experience in our new life in Christ.

THE REIGN OF GOD IN THE FUTURE

Having seen that God's reign has already begun in Jesus' life and teaching, we turn now to expectations of its future fulfillment. In treatments of the future reign, several terms recur and need to be explained.

The first term is eschatology or eschaton, which literally means the last things. The last things are the end of the world, the coming of Christ in glory and his judgment of all nations, eternal happiness for the just and eternal punishment for the unjust. Sometimes individual eschatology, i.e., what happens to me when I die, is distinguished from this general eschatology, since I may die before these cosmic events take place. In Christian writings on eschatology, we find references both to future eschatology and to present or realized eschatology, the end time as it has already commenced for those who live in Christ.

The second term is apocalyptic or apocalypse. Apocalyptic is a particular vision of eschatology, and a stylized literary genre in which the vision is expressed. There are apocalyptic passages in both the Hebrew and Christian scriptures, for example in Daniel 7-12, Ezekiel 1-9, and the book of Revelation.

> I gazed into the visions of the night.
> And I saw, coming on the clouds of heaven,
> one like a son of man.
> He came to the one of great age
> and was led into his presence.
> On him was conferred sovereignty,
> glory and kingship,
> and all peoples, nations and languages
> became his servants (Dan 7:13-14).

> In my vision, when he broke the sixth seal, there was a violent earthquake and the sun went as black as coarse sackcloth; the moon turned red as blood all over, and the stars of the sky fell on to the earth like figs dropping from a fig tree when a high wind shakes it; the sky disappeared like a scroll rolling up and all the mountains and islands were shaken from their places. Then all the earthly rulers, the governors and the commanders, the rich people and the men of influence, the whole population, slaves and citizens, took to the mountains to hide in caves and among the rocks (Rev 6:12-16).

Apocalyptic writing flourishes when times are particularly bad, and people can see no way out except through a dramatic intervention by God. Such literature was especially popular in Judaism from 200 B.C.E. to 200 C.E. The apocalyptic passages in the Christian scriptures, like the one from Revelation above, are not original creations, but borrow from a long tradition of religious imagery. Jesus himself, in his so-called "eschatological discourses" (Mk 13; Mt 24; Lk 21), merely passes on the apocalyptic tradition of his time, identifying the son of man spoken of in the tradition with himself.

A certain set language and imagery developed in apocalyptic literature. It involves world catastrophe, the supreme struggle of the powers of evil against God, and a dreadful combat in which they are finally defeated. It claims to be a revelation of the future, kept secret until the present. Much of this imagery has taken root in the popular imagination and comes readily to mind when we think of the last days: signs in the heavens such as the moon darkening and the sun giving no light, natural disasters such as earthquakes, wars and rumors of wars. Apocalyptic writers expect God's triumph to occur suddenly and dramatically. The point of their message is the triumph of good over evil by the power of God. The imagery they use is just that—imagery, the language of the imagination. Neither the beginning nor the end of history, the first things nor the last things, are accessible to human experience. Faced with the limits of reason, they use the suggestive power of poetry and story to express their hopes and fears regarding such things. It would be a mistake to read them as if they were giving a literal description of future events.

The second coming of Christ, also called the parousia (the Greek root means "presence" or "arrival"), is a central element in eschatological expectation. When is it supposed to take place? Christian writings reflect a variety of beliefs. Numerous texts suggest that it is imminent (Mt 10:23; 24:34; Mk 13:30; Lk 21:32). Some of the early communities expected Jesus to return during their own lifetime. Paul's converts in the Greek city of Thessalonica worry about the fate of those who might still be living when the parousia occurs. Some of them apparently see no reason to get jobs since Jesus is returning soon. They are not unlike Christians of later centuries who sell their goods and literally wait on hilltops. Paul tells them to get up and get to work (2 Thes 3:10-12). The proper attitudes toward Christ's second coming, he says, are patience, confident hope, mutual love, faith, and Christian living.

As time goes on, people settle in for a longer wait. They focus on the era of the church as a period of preparation for the parousia. The gospel of Luke, for example, while it does not deny imminent expectations, greatly deemphasizes them. Luke focuses on the role of the Spirit in the growth and continued existence of the church. Persecution and tribulation in Luke's gospel are not signs of the end, but part of the ongoing experience of Christian life. The second letter of Peter, probably written early in the second century, explains the delay of the Lord by a quotation from the psalms: "With the Lord one day is like a thousand years, a thousand years like one day."

Did the early Christians misunderstand Jesus in expecting his return so soon? Or was Jesus' knowledge limited or mistaken in this regard? Since the tradition that the time of the parousia is unknown is just as strong as the tradition of its imminence, it is difficult to give a simple answer to these questions. Jesus belonged to an apocalyptic generation which expected the reign of God soon. But he refused to give an exact date for the arrival of God's reign. He was not interested in revealing secret events or, more generally, in playing to mere human curiosity. His interest was in the decisive and practical matter of how to live. So he tells his disciples to be ready for the end always; the parousia will come without warning, like a thief in the night. This is the point of the parables of the wise and foolish virgins (Mt 25:1-13), the talents (Mt 25:14-30), and the pounds (Lk 19:11-27).

He stresses that God's future is hopeful and that, indeed, it has already come. He also tells his followers they have a decisive role to play in bringing it to fulfillment.

In light of his teachings, the questions we should be asking about the future are not when will the end come and what shape will it take, but what can we hope for from the God of Jesus, and how can we help to bring about God's reign today? On these more practical points, Jesus' teaching is clear. He affirms that whatever happens in history, God remains faithful and in the end will be fully victorious over evil. The traditional imagery by which he conveys some of this is not intended as an exact description of the course of events, but rather as a vivid depiction of the calamities and miseries of all ages, filled with the conviction that God triumphs in all things. "Now when these things begin to take place, look up and raise your heads, because your redemption is drawing near" (Lk 21:28).

THE FINAL JUDGMENT, HEAVEN, AND HELL

In discussing eschatology, we are speaking on two levels: 1) universal or collective eschatology, the present and future of the total human community and all of creation; and 2) individual eschatology, the future of individual persons within that universe. It is not only the end of the world that concerns us, but our own individual end or death as well. Many see death as the summation of all the other evils we fear, the ultimate threat to our existence. Reflection on the last things raises such questions as, Do we continue to exist beyond death, and, if so, in what way?

One way of explaining life after death has been to speak of the immortality of the soul. At death the body separates from the soul; the soul then lives on eternally. This is more a Greek than a Hebrew explanation, for it presupposes a dualistic notion of the human person as composed of body and soul, the soul being the more perfect, indestructible part. The biblical notion of the person is of a unity of body and spirit, so the biblical explanation of life after death involves the whole person, not just the soul. In answer to our question about *how* the dead exist, then, the bible speaks of the whole person continuing to live.

Many Christians have learned to think of both the end of the world and their personal death primarily in terms of the judgment of God and subsequent existence in heaven or hell. Mention of it evokes fear and anxiety. Perhaps it was used as a threat to get us to obey as children. In part, this notion of judgment is based on biblical references to the need for watchfulness and the coming of Christ in judgment on the last day, such as are found in the parable of the wheat and the weeds. In this story both good and evil are allowed to coexist until the end of the world when the weeds will be gathered up and burned, and the just will shine like the sun in the kingdom (Mt 13:36-43). What meaning do these ideas have for us today?

Just as we are accustomed to think of the kingdom of God as a place or a geographical territory, so we have learned to think of heaven and hell as places or regions above and below the earth. Most Christian theology today rejects such spatial understandings. Heaven and hell can also be misunderstood if they are seen as rewards or punishments imposed from without, decisions about our future determined by a judging God who has weighed our every action in the balance. Contemporary explanations of heaven and hell focus rather on the meaning of human freedom in relation to God's free offer of love. Within such a perspective, the reality of hell is a way of acknowledging that human persons can choose to make themselves miserable forever. We can reject the compassion and forgiveness of God which scripture portrays as unlimited. We can refuse to be united with God, a refusal that is permanent with death. But that refusal is our choice, not God's punishment. Since we are made for God and for others, to be closed in on ourselves without contact with God and others is to be lost forever. The doctrine of hell reveals the terrible human potential for self-destruction. Scripture expresses this through images such as darkness, gnashing of teeth, and fire. Most scripture commentators consider these references to be part of the apocalyptic rhetoric of Jesus' era. They aptly capture the experience of being cut off, lost, missing the end and purpose of existence.

We do not know whether anyone will experience the final loss of salvation. Out of respect for the reality of human freedom we must reckon with the possibility, but we do not know whether any individual has in fact made this choice. The French novelist, Georges Bernanos, once remarked that hell means "not to love anymore." That comes as close to a description as we can get.

Statements about heaven, on the other hand, describe the fulfillment and happiness of those who choose God and love. Heaven too is the final fruit of what we have made of ourselves through our choices in response to God's invitations. It is not a reward suddenly bestowed. Scripture describes this future with God in numerous images: as a banquet, as being in God's house, as the community of all who have reached their fulfillment, as a glorious day which will never end. Since we have been created to be together, Jesus' statements about the resurrection on the last day refer primarily to humanity and creation as a whole. Resurrection is a social event. We long for this time when the human community along with all the rest of creation can live together in friendship, justice, and peace.

Something of this joy begins already in this life. We therefore get some sense of what transformed existence might be by looking at those aspects of our experience which provide a taste and promise of the eternal. Karl Rahner suggests that something of eternity is contained, for example, in every radical affirmation of love. Our longing for the ultimate is another foretaste of the future. We reach out continually beyond limits. We never find enough love, truth, freedom, beauty, goodness, or joy in this life. Heaven names the final fulfillment of this unquenchable longing and hope. It brings to fruition the seeds of indestructibility existing in every human heart.

THE END OF THE WORLD AND CHRISTIAN DISCIPLESHIP

The kingdom comes mainly by an act of God. This is clear throughout scripture. We do not usher in the reign of God either by our wisdom or by our folly. But our attitude toward the last things has a strong effect on how we feel and live. It can fill us with fatalism or create the energy and hope we need to invest ourselves in what God is doing to bring creation to fulfillment. What is the relationship between our expectation of the reign of God and our Christian task? One aspect of this relationship is the realization that our concrete love of others and the earth is the way we love God. The world is not merely a stopping-off place on our way to God. Our love of other creatures has eternal significance and validity. In fact, all that we do in this world has meaning and importance for the new creation.

The future world does not stand in complete separation from this world, as though God were concerned only with the hereafter and we are simply to put up with this world until then. God is deeply invested in the development of this world, which is the matrix of the future kingdom. What this means for us is that the hour of decision is now. Hope in the future enables us to criticize and transform the present world in light of Jesus' teaching, to face and overcome those problems which threaten our future. The time for conversion and the investment of our own energy is now.

SUMMARY

Christians of every era have been interested in calculating the exact time of the second coming of Christ which will usher in the final things: the end of the world, judgment, heaven and hell. Jesus, however, discourages such speculation, telling us instead to live every moment as if it might be our last. We are to be ready at any time for his coming. Moreover, God's reign has already begun and is in our midst.

The apocalyptic passages in the bible describe in vivid imagery the final struggle between the powers of good and evil. The imagery is not to be taken literally. The message is one of hope for the final fulfillment of God's reign and the victory of good over evil.

While we help to bring it about, the blessed future promised us is finally God's gift. Jesus' message about the future is one of hope and love. Heaven is the happiness promised to all who open themselves to God and love; hell is the pain which results from a permanent refusal to love.

Questions and Exercises

1. What ideas and attitudes do you have about the end of the world? Where did you get them?

2. Describe the reign or kingdom of God as you understand it from Jesus' life and teachings. Indicate both its present and future meanings.

3. Explain: a) eschatology, b) apocalytic, and c) parousia. What examples from literature other than the bible can you find—

e.g., poetry, songs, advertising—of imagery that conveys a message but is not meant to be taken literally?

4. Are attempts to establish an exact timetable for the last days in accord with Jesus' message? What attitudes should a Christian have toward the second coming?

5. What are your convictions about life after death? How do you respond to the descriptions of heaven and hell presented in this chapter?

6. Examine your own life for any experiences that might confirm Karl Rahner's suggestion that we already have in this life a taste and promise of the eternal.

7. Given the biblical understanding of the reign of God, what is the Christian's task in face of the contemporary world situation?

Suggestions for Further Reading

Adela Yarbo Collins, *Crisis and Catharsis: The Power of the Apocalypse* (Westminster, 1984). A New Testament scholar uses history, sociology, anthropology, and psychology to bring fresh light to the book of Revelation.

James H. Evans, Jr., *We Have Been Believers: An African-American Systematic Theology* (Fortress, 1992). Brings black religious experience to several areas of theology, including the meaning of eschatology and hope.

Wilfred Harrington, *Revelation* (Liturgical Press, 1993). A detailed and helpful commentary on the book of Revelation.

Zachary Hayes, *Visions of a Future: A Study of Christian Eschatology* (Liturgical Press, 1989). A comprehensive treatment of the end of the world, heaven and hell, and the relationship between the historical action of building the world and the reign of God.

John Hick, *Death and Eternal Life* (Westminster, 1994). An

interdisciplinary study of the mystery of death and eschatology as found in the major religions.

Marjorie Hewitt Suchocki, *God, Christ, Church: A Practical Guide to Process Theology* (Crossroad, 1982). Presents an understanding of eschatology that flows from process theology's understanding of God's power and kingdom.

Jerry L. Walls, *Hell: The Logic of Damnation* (University of Notre Dame, 1993). Examines historical beliefs about hell and damnation, and presents some modern interpretations.

CHAPTER 13

Christianity Among the Religions of the World

Christians account for only about one-third of the world's population today. Jews, Hindus, Muslims, and Buddhists make up most of the rest, giving us five major living religions. There are, of course, many people who belong to still other religions, as well as countless agnostics and atheists who have not aligned themselves with any religion. Until the latter half of the present century, the Christian attitude was that Christians were the only genuinely religious people, and that all others, in bondage to various kinds of error, constituted a vast field for potential conversions. Now after two thousand years of missionary endeavors, Christians are puzzled to find themselves still a minority. In the immortal words of Canon Max Warren, general secretary of the World Missionary Society, "We have marched around alien Jerichos the requisite number of times. We have sounded the trumpets. And the walls have not collapsed."

The situation raises several questions for the Christian: 1) What role, if any, does Jesus Christ play in the salvation of non-Christians? 2) If there is one God, why are there so many religions? 3) What sort of stance should Christians take toward non-Christians?

JESUS CHRIST AND THE SALVATION OF NON-CHRISTIANS

Is it possible to be saved without faith in Jesus? The term "salvation" has many meanings. The most crucial sense of it for the present discussion is life after death. The blunt question then is whether a person can get to heaven without faith in Jesus. A second question would be whether a person could enjoy the benefits of some kind of salvation in this world without Jesus, i.e., some kind of contact with God, some experience of God's graciousness (the meaning of the term "grace"), some help with the problems of the human situation.

There are two basic positions on how crucial Jesus is in bringing human beings salvation. One is that all salvation comes from him and him alone. The other is that he is just one among many mediators of salvation. Each of these two basic positions has some shadings, which we will examine in the course of our development.

Jesus Christ Is the Exclusive Mediator of God's Salvation

This position has a long tradition among Christians and can claim a number of scripture texts in its support.

> And Jesus said to them: "Go into all the world and preach the good news to all creation. The person who believes and is baptized will be saved; the person who does not believe will be condemned" (Mk 16:15-16).

> "Furthermore, there is no salvation in anyone else, for there is not another name under heaven that has been given to human beings by which we must be saved" (Acts 4:12, sermon by Peter).

> Jesus said: "I am the way and the truth and the life. No one comes to the Father except through me" (Jn 14:6).

> For there is one God, and one mediator between God
> and human beings, the man Jesus Christ (1 Tim 2:5).

The conviction that Christianity is the one true religion, and sometimes even more exclusively that the Roman Catholic Church is the one true church, has led to great missionary efforts throughout the world in all the Christian centuries. The conviction has led, less happily, to competitions, persecutions, religious wars, and the use of bribery or force to bring conversions. The underlying theology has various shadings.

1) The most exclusive reading of it is that one must be explicitly a member of the church, and so one must be baptized. This too has scriptural underpinnings. In addition to the Marcan text cited above, there is the Johannine text:

> Jesus answered: "Most truly I say to you, unless a person
> is born again from water and the spirit, they cannot
> enter the kingdom of God" (Jn 3:3. The expression
> "born again Christian" originates here).

To name but one Christian missionary who worked out of this theology, St. Francis Xavier in the sixteenth century spent his life among the people of the Orient, giving basic Christian instruction and baptizing. A man of tremendous zeal and energy, he moved through India and Japan, and died off the coast of mainland China, his next great project. He was driven by a consuming love for Christ. But by his own admission, he worked out of the conviction that by baptism he was snatching as many souls as he could from hell.

2) A less exclusive position holds that persons might be saved outside the Christian church, but that the salvation which reaches them is mediated through the church, because all salvation comes through Christ and he

extends it to people through the church. This theology may or may not speculate on how that salvation reaches people who are not members of the church. One theory is that the church has at least to some extent Christianized human culture.

3) A still less exclusive position holds that salvation is ultimately from Christ, but that it reaches some people quite without the mediation of the church. Thus it is not necessary either to be a member of the church or even to be culturally under the influence of the church. Christ can reach people with his grace independently of the church. This theology does not usually explain how. It relies implicitly on an identification of Christ with God. As God is omnipresent, so is Christ. Where God is active, Christ is active.

What all three of these variant positions have in common is the proposition that all salvation comes through Christ. They differ in the degree of involvement of the church as the mediation of Christ's salvation.

Difficulties with the Exclusivist Position

Some theologians today are abandoning this exclusivist position and moving to the more open stance that Jesus is only one mediator of salvation among others. There are essentially three considerations that persuade them to do this.

1) The first is the realization that there are many good people who lie outside the Christian sphere. When Christians live in their own ghettos, they do not have significant contact with these people. But when under conditions of modern mobility these ghettos dissolve and people of all kinds are mixed together, a puzzling experience breaks in quite powerfully. One works next to a

professed atheist who is a person of high moral quality. One goes to school with a Jew, Hindu, or Muslim who is not only morally upright but religiously devout. These people seem to have a lively relationship with God. How can this be? They do not draw their inspiration from Jesus; they may know very little of him, and feel no need to learn more. Yet they live very impressive lives, sometimes better lives than Christians live.

2) The second experience is noted by those who study comparative religion. They read the scriptures of other religions and dialogue with their members. The sacred writings seem genuinely inspired and uplifting. The ethics stressed in the teachings of the non-Christian religions are essentially the same as the ethics found in the teachings of Christianity, and they are lived in similar ways. Dogmas differ, rituals differ, but the ways of life observable across the religious spectrum do not show significant differences. A spiritual person of one tradition has no difficulty recognizing a spiritual person of another.

3) The third consideration is the conundrum of the world religious picture in the late twentieth century. The world is about one-third Christian, about one-sixth Roman Catholic. If you take the exclusivist position that salvation is attainable only by faith in Jesus, two-thirds of humanity is damned; five-sixths if your requirement is Roman Catholicism. This raises an acute question about God: What kind of God is it who creates the vast majority of human beings for eternal damnation? Don't Christians preach a God of love? Are all these people fully responsible for the fact that they are not Christians?

These are the main considerations which lead to the more open Christian position on salvation, to which we now turn.

Jesus Christ Is One Mediator of Salvation Among Others

What many Christians do not realize is that this position too can appeal to texts of scripture.

> At this Peter opened his mouth and said: "For a certainty I perceive that God shows no partiality, but in every nation the person that fears God and does what is right is acceptable to God" (Acts 10:34).

> "As I walked about looking at your shrines, I even discovered an altar inscribed 'To a God Unknown.'" What you are worshiping without knowing it, that I proclaim to you" (Acts 17:23, Paul's sermon to the Greeks).

> When Gentiles who do not have the law keep it as by instinct, these people although without the law serve as a law for themselves. They show that the demands of the law are written in their hearts. Their conscience bears witness together with the law, and their thoughts will accuse or defend them on the day when, in accordance with the gospel I preach, God will pass judgment on the secrets of human beings through Christ Jesus (Rom 2:14-16).

> God wants all persons to be saved and come to the knowledge of the truth (1 Tim 2:3-4).

> This explains why we work and struggle as we do; our hopes are fixed on the living God who is the savior of *all* persons, but *especially* of those who believe (1 Tim 4:10, italics ours).

> God is love, and those who abide in love abide in God and God in them (1 Jn 4:16).

These texts loosen the hold of the exclusivist position and of the fear or fanaticism which sometimes attend that position. You will recall that scripture contains various theological viewpoints. These texts depict a God whose salvific intent is universal, and the signs of whose saving action are perceivable in persons outside the Christian community, perhaps even outside the whole scope of Jesus' influence.

One could hold this sort of latitude about salvation and still maintain that where there is salvation it is due to the influence of Jesus even if he is not recognized. But theologians of a more empirical cast of mind find this position unconvincing. They see no evidence that it comes from Jesus. They take seriously the testimony of the people concerned, who say they never heard of Jesus or at least that he is no real factor in their lives. These people draw their religious inspiration from other sources. Thus it seems that Jesus is one mediator of God's salvation among others.

There are two variations of this basic position.

1) The first holds that although Jesus Christ is not the exclusive mediator, he is the normative mediator. This means that he is the highest, the fullest, the most complete, and hence the norm by which all other mediations are to be measured. This is the position Paul Tillich takes. There is in Jesus a unique fullness of God and salvation. All other forms of salvation are only approximations, falling in some measure short and needing to be filled out or corrected by his, though they are sufficient for salvation in individual cases. This position usually bases itself on the strong claims scripture makes for Jesus and his relationship with God. Sometimes it also attempts to show from a comparative study of all the religions that the Christian religion is particularly rich, balanced, and inclusive of all that is true and good in the other religions.

2) The other variation of the one-among-many position holds that Jesus is indeed a mediator of salvation but that it cannot be shown that he is superior to the others and

therefore normative. He may be, but no human being is competent to evaluate all the religious founders and their religious systems and declare which is the greatest. The Christian scriptures represent a particular point of view. They are culturally situated and limited in their horizon, and cannot rise to a universal standpoint. The contemporaries of Jesus did not know the whole world and its many cultures so that they could situate Jesus among them. Their statements are necessarily relative, as all human statements are, even those in which divine inspiration is a component. As far as the statements of comparative religionists are concerned, those people who have found Christ and Christianity to be the greatest have all been Christians. Their objectivity may be called into question. Also, if Christianity were truly the richest and most balanced religion, wouldn't the other religions in 2000 years' time have come to recognize this fact and converge on it as the center? This has not happened, and does not seem to be happening.

Theological Underpinnings of the More Open Position

Karl Rahner is well known for his theology of implicit or anonymous Christianity. It is derived from the two basic concepts of his total theology: the human person as the mystery of infinite emptiness and God as the mystery of infinite fullness. God is the horizon in the life of every person, experienced at the edges of consciousness. God reaches out graciously to every person, and is at least dimly known by every person as that mysterious power in human life that both challenges and comforts. Whenever anyone opens to that mystery and responds to it in attitudes and choices, that person displays faith, even if he or she does not acknowledge God or Christ by name. By what signs can we know that someone has this implicit faith? It shows itself in hope and love. Those who have it are hopeful even in the midst of adversity. They continue to believe that life is worth living, that it still makes sense to move forward into tomorrow, that things will somehow work out. And at least in some measure they love." They apply themselves to their daily responsibilities, take care of their families, transcend selfishness in their relationships with at least some people. By these manifestations of hope and love, we know the presence of their implicit faith or yes-saying to God.

In the vast majority of human lives, we find hope and love at least in some measure. In Jesus we find them most fully, because his was the fullest correspondence with God. Even in the lives of *explicit* Christians, the call is no different or greater than to live out our faith as fully as possible in hope and love. What more is there? Any scripture passage will be found to be exhorting us either to hope or to love. So God's program for implicit and explicit Christians is the same, but explicit Christians have many advantages in living it out precisely because their faith is fully conscious and its supports are more abundant and tangible.

Rahner's name of "anonymous Christian" or "implicit Christian" for those who respond to God's gracious outreach in their lives without an explicit Christian commitment has come under criticism. It does not appeal to those who are so named, any more than it would appeal to a Christian to be called an "anonymous Buddhist." Most of us prefer to have our self-descriptions taken seriously. We feel fairly sure we know what we are, and being told we are really something else sounds patronizing.

But the difficulty may be deeper than diplomacy. Rahner is persuaded that there is only one mediator, Jesus, through whom all grace comes. Thus, even though there is no empirical evidence that those whose lives exhibit hope and love are under the influence of Jesus, Rahner holds that they are. Other theologians see it differently. Not everything that comes from God has to come through Jesus, because the reality of God is not exhausted in the reality of Jesus. Jesus is an *historical* reality. There is a life, a teaching, a scripture, an institution—all in the concrete historical order. Some people come within this ambience and open to it. Others do not. There is no real justification for calling the latter Christians, and no need to. For God's relationship to the world through Word and Spirit is larger than the incarnation in Jesus of Nazareth. There have been other historical persons in whom God's Word has been eloquently spoken, other scriptures in which the Spirit of God has been manifestly at work, and other historical institutions which embody these influences. Besides these, there is the depth of every human heart, that private, silent region which is plumbed by the Spirit of God. Jesus is but one avenue to God, even if he be the principal one.

WHY ARE THERE SO MANY RELIGIONS?

If there is only one God, why are there so many religions? In the past Christian theology has tended to regard non-Christian religions as mere superstitions, human fabrications hardly worth a second thought, whereas the Christian religion has all been revealed by God. But the considerations summarized in this chapter have called that attitude into question, and led for the first time to a serious grappling with the phenomenon of humankind's religious diversity. Experiences like the following put the matter in sharpest focus.

William Johnston, an American-born Roman Catholic priest, has worked for years in Japan with a particular interest in promoting dialogue between Christianity and Zen Buddhism. In the introduction to his book, *The Still Point*,

Johnston recounts how when Christians and Buddhists gathered for a week of dialogue in Kyoto in 1968, deep and lasting friendships were formed. The atmosphere was one of understanding and charity. When all sat in silent meditation, there was a palpable sense of their unity with the Mystery and one another. When it came to values, the values that flow from contemplation, they found themselves in total agreement. All prized deep meditation, simplicity of life, humility, gratitude, truthfulness, mindfulness, non-violence, and peacemaking, and wished to collaborate with one another to improve the human condition. The stumbling block came when they tried to formulate some philosophical or theological statements on which all could agree. There were none. This same experience has happened to many others. It seems that mysticism, spiritual values, and practical collaboration unite the adherents of the various religions, whereas theology divides. Why should this be?

1) *Karl Rahner: Transcendental and Categorical Revelation*

Rahner explains that there is always a gap between the actual experience of the transcendent God (transcendental revelation) and the attempt to express that experience in human categories of understanding (categorical revelation). Because we experience God as a mystery beyond our comprehension, our attempts to give expression to what that mystery is and what it means for us to align ourselves with it necessarily fall short of the transcendent experience itself. These attempts are inadequate, even groping, and most often expressed in symbolic language (stories, poetry, symbols, myth) which is difficult to pin down conceptually.

The consequence is that there are various religions, each inspired by the religious experience and articulation of a particular gifted individual or individuals. The religions show diversity in the way the transcendent mystery is imaged or conceptualized, in the way rituals for relating to it are created, and to some extent in the way ethical requirements for living in harmony with it are proclaimed. These human modes of interpretation and expression are bound to be influenced by the cultural setting in which they are created. There results considerable variety, and yet also some constants. What Rahner is showing in his distinction between transcendental and categorical revelation is that God does not dictate to us the words, images, or stories which later come to be sacred scripture or "divine revelation" in a given religious tradition. God's revelation always comes through a human mediator, and shows all the cultural particularity of that mediation. It is revelation, but in a divine/human blend.

2) *Wilfred Cantwell Smith: Faith and Belief*

Another explanation of religious diversity comes from Wilfred Cantwell Smith, an American Protestant historian of religion. As he surveys the religious scene, he sees a fundamental difference between faith and beliefs. Faith is the primary religious category, running through all the religions. It is the decision to open one's life to the Mystery. Belief has often been confused with it, particularly in the last few centuries, but in reality belief is secondary, derivative, and in some religious traditions not very important. Belief is the attempt to put into intelligible statement what that mystery is to which one gives oneself in faith.

The root meaning of the term "faith" in Latin (*credo*) is "to give one's heart" (*cor do*). So it means to set one's heart on, to cherish, to put one's trust in. In the bible, this is the fundamental human response to the transcendent. In Hinduism there is a core term that not only has the same meaning, but a parallel etymology, the word *sraddha*. It is a compound of Sanskrit *srad* (heart) and *dha* (to put). The Qur'an (sometimes written Koran, the scriptures of Islam), while it has no term for "belief," has a frequently recurring word for "faith," *amana*, which has very much the same meaning as *credo* and *sraddha*: engagement, commitment, recognition of and submission to God.

Beliefs, implicit or explicit, are of course involved in the commitment of faith. But they are not primary. That is why Smith finds so inadequate the first question habitually asked by Christians about some other religion, "What do they believe?"

Smith goes further. It is not primarily on religions that we ought to focus anyway, he says. It is on *persons*. Religions are objective, impersonal, of centuries-long standing. They are cumulative traditions with many elements: scriptures, laws, rituals, buildings, myths, symbols, priesthoods, hierarchies, doctrines. We can study all these things and miss the person who lives within them. Do we know what a Roman Catholic is when we have studied Roman Catholic history, doctrine, rituals? No, Smith says. It is persons we must study, and the only way to study them is to talk and walk with them. Our questions then are: What does it feel like to be a Jew, a Buddhist, a Muslim? How do you view the universe, yourself, other people, the transcendent? What do you make of relationships, death, sexuality, work, suffering, pleasure? How would you express life's deepest values? How do you conduct yourself in the world? When we begin to ask questions like these, and ask them of persons, we begin really to get at the meaning of an individual's or community's engagement with the transcendent.

Interestingly, the attempt to express that lived reality in the form of beliefs, Smith points out, is something that has interested Christians (Roman Catholics particularly) more than it has the adherents of any other religion. In other religions, the myth or the ritual or meditation or the ethical path is more important than doctrine. Christianity has put a particular emphasis on beliefs or doctrines, the intellectual articulation and systematization of the elements of its relationship with God. This is a fact of which Christians were not even aware until the dialogue with non-Christians gave them a broader perspective. The new awareness challenges them to reflect on the relative importance of beliefs and on their validity as truth claims.

In sum, we gain some insight into the puzzle of human-kind's religious diversity when we grasp the distinction between experience of the transcendent and the human articulation of that experience, between mysticism and doctrine, between faith as personal engagement with mystery and beliefs as intellectual expression of that engagement. Each religion is a unique divine/human blend.

THE CHRISTIAN STANCE TOWARD NON-CHRISTIANS

In the contemporary situation of religious diversity, what should the Christian stance toward non-Christians be?

Many Christian theologians, church leaders, and Christians at large seem to be coming to a significantly different stance than before. They are moving away from the attitude that they alone know the true God and serve God the way it should be done, away from the assumption that others are involved in mere superstition and error. The new attitude is one of positive appreciation and genuine curiosity, prompting an open exchange with others in the conviction that others have much to teach as well as new things to learn.

Does Christian evangelization, the attempt to spread the gospel, still make sense today? To Christians of the exclusivist persuasion, it still makes perfect sense and is an urgent responsibility. To those who see God's saving work in the world as broader than the Christian framework, evangelization still makes sense, but it is carried on with a somewhat different understanding and purpose. The motive is not to save souls from hell. It is not even primarily to make converts to the Christian religion, though converts are always welcome. The purpose is simply to share the good news of Jesus and to live the Christian life among and for other people. Good news cries out to be shared. Christians are enthusiasts, people who have found a treasure buried in a field (Mt 13:44) and want to share it with others. Christians are also compassionate, and where they see people suffering, or in need, they want to render all possible help. Thus Christian evangelization and mission will always be both valid and important.

And if people do not respond by joining the church? This does not mean Christian efforts were in vain. If people have seen genuine Christian living, they have almost certainly been affected in some way for the better. They have probably been moved to be better Hindus, Jews, Muslims, Buddhists, or "atheists." The leaven has been mixed with the dough and is working there (Mt 13:33), even if we cannot perceive all its effects. What is more, the Christians in the encounter have probably also been moved to be better Christians by the influence of genuinely good people of other faiths.

The growing dialogue among the religions has enriched Christianity as a whole in myriad ways. Christians have incorporated many of the attitudes and practices of eastern and Islamic mysticism into their prayer, and found their prayer the richer for it. This has led to a renewed interest in the Christian mystical tradition and prompted us to make it more widely available than before. Christians have learned yoga and found it beneficial for body and mind, a fine preparation particularly for contemplation. The I-Thou thinking of Jewish writer Martin Buber has deepened our relationships with God and one another. Contact with Mohandas Gandhi and his non-violent approach to social and political change has gotten us back in touch with the non-violence in our own scriptures, and shown us how to put it into action. These are just a few examples of the enrichment that has taken place. The growing dialogue and cross-fertilization stands in marked contrast with the attitudes of the not too distant past, as portrayed in the following parable.

> My friend and I went to the fair, the World Fair of Religions. Not a trade fair. A religion fair. But the competition was as fierce, the propaganda as loud.
>
> At the Jewish stall, we were given handouts that said God was all-compassionate and the Jews were his Chosen People. The Jews. No other people were chosen.
>
> At the Muslim stall, we learned that God was all-merciful and Mohammed is his only Prophet. There is no salvation except in listening to this Prophet.
>
> At the Christian stall, we discovered that God is Love and there is no salvation outside the Church. Join the Church or be damned.
>
> On the way out I asked my friend, "What do you think of God?" She replied, "The picture I get is that God is bigoted, and cruel. But it is very hard to figure out whose side God is really on."

If the religions want to compete today, says Wilfred Cantwell Smith, let them outdo one another in their spirit of reconciliation and their labors to bring about a better world. When religious diversity leads to walls of separation, mutual calumny, persecution, and war, one must wonder, as many nonbelievers do, whether religion is a help or a hindrance.

Surely conciliation and collaboration would be the spirit of Jesus were he in the flesh for the dialogue of the religions today. Such was his attitude two thousand years ago when he blessed the good wherever he encountered it—in the Syro-Phoenician woman (Mk 7), the Roman centurion (Mt 8), and the Samaritan woman (Jn 4), all of whom lay outside the pale of orthodox belief.

Christians can have this open and appreciative stance without losing anything of their own love of Jesus or their total dedication to being Christian. There is nothing incompatible between commitment and openness. The openness called for is not a relativism which conduces to indifference or paralysis. Christians can remain steadfastly and enthusiastically on the path they have found salvific, even while recognizing there are other paths as well.

SUMMARY

There are two basic positions taken by Christian theologians on the question of Jesus' role in the salvation of all people. One is that he is the only mediator of salvation. The other is that he is one among many. Each of these positions has various shadings. At the present time, the experience of living with persons of other traditions, the study of comparative religion, and reflection on the religious situation after two centuries of Christian mission are causing many theologians to move to a more open position.

Humankind's religious diversity finds helpful explanation in distinctions between transcendental and categorical revelation and between faith and beliefs. Actual dialogue with persons of other religions seems a better avenue to religious understanding and enrichment than the study of religious traditions in the abstract.

Christian evangelization will always be a meaningful and important activity, wherever one stands on the question of salvation. For many Christians today, evangelization operates out of broader assumptions and shows a different approach. That persons from other traditions likewise have much to offer Christians is already a matter of experience.

Questions and Exercises

1. Summarize the various positions taken by Christian theologians in their assessment of the role Jesus plays in the salvation of non-Christians. What is the reasoning behind each position?

2. What is your position on the above question, and the reasons for it?

3. If there is one God, why are there so many religions?

4. Explain the distinction between transcendental and categorical revelation, and that between faith and beliefs. What light do these distinctions shed on religious diversity?

5. What stance should Christians take toward non-Christians? What sense, if any, does Christian mission make in today's world?

6. How is it possible to be both a committed Christian and someone open to other religious ideas?

7. Initiate a dialogue with someone of a different faith. See what you find out about that person's view of the world and human existence. What are your reflections?

8. Read a book which presents a non-Christian religion sympathetically. What are your reflections?

Suggestions for Further Reading

Tosh Arai and Wesley Ariarajah, eds., *Spirituality in Interfaith Dialogue* (Orbis, 1990). Personal testimonies of Christians who have lived in dialogue with people of other faiths and integrated new disciplines into their own spirituality.

Paula Cooey et al., eds., *After Patriarchy: Feminist Transformations of the World Religions* (Orbis, 1991). An anthology of essays by women seeking sexism-transcending, life-giving elements in the various traditions.

Bede Griffiths, *Universal Wisdom: A Journey through the Sacred Wisdom of the World* (HarperSanFrancisco, 1994). A collection of sacred texts from eight religious traditions, showing the deep connections between them, by a Roman Catholic priest who lived his life in an ashram in India.

John Hick and Paul Knitter, eds., *The Myth of Christian Uniqueness* (Orbis, 1987). A collection of essays in which Christian theologians debate the role of Jesus vis-à-vis the salvation of all persons.

Arvind Sharma, ed., *Our Religions* (HarperSanFrancisco, 1994). Seven living world religions are introduced by preeminent scholars from each tradition.

Arvind Sharma, ed., *Women in World Religions* (Albany: State University of New York Press, 1987). Feminist theologians examine the world's religious traditions and evaluate their attitudes toward women.

Huston Smith, *The World's Religions*. Revised edition (HarperSanFrancisco, 1994). A sympathetic account of what it is like to live within each of seven different religious traditions.

Wilfred Cantwell Smith, *Religious Diversity* (Crossroad, 1982). A series of essays written over sixteen years on the world religious situation, advocating new approaches to Christian mission and the study of religious traditions.

Leonard Swidler, ed., *Toward a Universal Theology of Religion* (Orbis, 1987). A collection of essays in which eminent scholars from the world's major religious traditions grapple with the problem of religious diversity.

Conclusion

This book's first chapter was an encounter with the riddle of existence, especially as it presents itself at the dawn of the third millennium. It is clear that the world stands in great need, crisis even. It is also evident that in each individual life, there will always be a quest for meaning and purpose, for true value and direction, for help to peace with self and harmony with all other beings. Now that we have reviewed the essential elements of the Christian program, it seems reasonable to conclude that it has much to offer us in our struggle with the problems and challenges of existence.

The figure of Jesus, his life and teaching, Christianity's best treasure, will stand forever as inspiration and summons. To relate to God through him puts us in touch with our salvation and our peace.

To follow him clearly demands something of us. We may have to give up some of our "pleasures," or at least our excesses. We may need to become more generous in sharing our goods. We may need to open more to others generally—to be more interested, more respectful, more tolerant of difference, more forgiving of injuries. We may have to learn to be more patient with and accepting of ourselves. We may have to be more respectful of nature in all its manifestations and gifts, and take less from it. As the vital source of this whole new way of seeing and being, we may need to give more time to personal prayer, communal worship, and the kind of reading that nourishes the spirit and causes it to expand.

In exchange, we would be enriched out of all proportion to what we had "given up." We would be more at peace with ourselves and far richer in relationship. We would have more satisfaction and sense of purpose in life, experience more growth, find more fulfillment.

Let us look beyond ourselves and think for a moment of the whole world. Suppose such ideas caught fire, and Christianity finally had its proper impact on the entire human situation. Wealth would be redistributed so that everyone had enough. Bigotry, hatred, and the persecution of minorities would end. There would be far less loneliness, because there would be much more community. Mental illness would be greatly reduced. Drugs would lose their appeal. There would be very few lawsuits, as the vast majority of disputes would be settled through dialogue and negotiation. War would be eliminated. Negotiation and fair compromises would take its place. There would be no more refugees. Crime would be practically eliminated. Who would need it, or want it? People would be far less interested in the exploitation of nature and the pursuit of wealth and power, far more interested in the welfare of all beings and the richness of the resulting community.

Does this sound like a dream? Yes—because it is a dream. It is Jesus' dream. He called it the reign of God.

Bibliography

Besides the books cited in individual chapters, the following works have influenced the writing of this book.

María Pilar Aquino, *Our Cry for Life: Feminist Theology for Latin America* (Orbis, 1993).

Rudolph Bultmann, *Theology of the New Testament* (Scribner's, 1951 and 1955).

Joseph Campbell, *Masks of God* (4 vols) (Penguin, 1976).

Anne Carr, *Transforming Grace: Christian Tradition and Women's Experience* (Harper, 1988).

Avery Dulles, *The Survival of Dogma* (Doubleday, 1971).,

Elisabeth Schüssler Fiorenza, *Bread Not Stone: The Challenge of Feminist Biblical Interpretation* (Beacon, 1984).

Elisabeth Schüssler Fiorenza, *In Memory of Her: A Feminist Theological Reconstruction of Christian Origins* (Crossroad, 1983).

Hans-Georg Gadamer, *Truth and Method* (Seabury, 1975).

David Griffin, *God, Power, and Evil: A Process Theodicy* (Westminster, 1976).

Gustavo Gutiérrez, *A Theology of Liberation*. Revised edition (Orbis, 1988).

Hans Küng, *On Being a Christian* (Crossroad, 1994).

Bernard Lee, ed., *Alternative Futures for Worship* (7 vols) (Collegeville, 1987).

Bernard Lonergan, *Method in Theology* (Herder, 1972).

Richard McBrien, *Catholicism*. Revised edition (Harper-SanFrancisco, l994).

Harding Meyer and Lukas Vischer, eds., *Growth in Agreement: Reports and Agreed Statements of Ecumenical Conversations on a World Level* (Paulist, 1984).

H. Richard Niebuhr, *Christ and Culture* (Harper, 1951).

Jaroslav Pelikan, *Jesus through the Centuries: His Place in the History of Culture* (Harper, 1985).

Karl Rahner, *Foundations of Christian Faith* (Crossroad, 1978).

Karl Rahner, *Theological Investigations* (Herder, many volumes, various topics).

Paul Ricoeur, *Interpretation Theory: Discourse and the Surplus of Meaning* (Texas Christian University, 1976).

Rosemary Radford Ruether, *Sexism and God-Talk: Toward a Feminist Theology* (Beacon, 1983).

Edward Schillebeeckx, *Church: The Human Story of God* (Crossroad, 1990).

Edward Schillebeeckx, *Jesus and Christ* (Crossroad, 1979 and 1981).

Dorothy Soelle, *Strength of the Weak: Toward a Christian Feminist Identity* (Westminster, 1984).

Charlene Spretnak, *States of Grace: The Recovery of Meaning in the Postmodern Age* (HarperSanFrancisco, 1991).

Paul Tillich, *Systematic Theology* (University of Chicago, 1967).

Alfred North Whitehead, *Process and Reality* (Macmillan, 1929).

Index